Sew on the Go

BY THE SAME AUTHOR

Chic on a Shoestring: Simple to Sew Vintage-style Accessories
The Modern Girl's Guide to Hatmaking: Fabulous Hats and Headbands
to Fashion at Home

Sew on the Go

A Maker's Journey

Mary Jane Baxter

Illustrations by Sarah Knight

unbound

First published in 2021

Unbound
TC Group, Level 1, Devonshire House, One Mayfair Place, London W1J 8AJ
www.unbound.com

Text design by PDQ Digital Media Solutions Ltd

A CIP record for this book is available from the British Library

ISBN 978-1-78352-916-2 (trade hbk)
ISBN 978-1-78352-917-9 (ebook)

Printed in Great Britain by CPI Group (UK)

1 3 5 7 9 8 6 4 2

Sew on the Go is a book about determination, inspiration, laughter and loneliness. It is also about creative and physical freedom, a freedom that both Brexit and the global coronavirus pandemic have sorely tested. I took the freedom to travel for granted and have recently been reminded that it is an enormous privilege.

Let us make every mile matter.

This book is dedicated to the Hosking Houses Trust, with thanks for all its support.

Mary Jane Baxter

You set off thinking you know the way,
And point yourself in the right direction.
At first, the road is clear,
You feel elated.

Free.

As time passes, doubt sets in. The path
No longer as straight as it seemed.
There are endless twists and turns.
Unexpected obstacles are scattered everywhere.

You keep on going. Hoping that
Somewhere down the line
You'll calibrate your compass
And set your sights on True North.

But has it crossed your mind that the goal may
Have shifted?
Has your South replaced your North?
Is your East now your West?

Things change.

To get your bearings, you must
Stop. Look. Listen.
Stay alert for that still small voice,
The one that will help you find your heart
And finally lead you home.

Mary Jane Baxter

Contents

Sew on the Go

Introduction

This book is based on a journey I made around Europe in my Mobile Makery – aka Bambi – my vintage camper van turned quirky craft studio on wheels. This is my third book. My previous titles, *Chic on a Shoestring* and *The Modern Girl's Guide to Hatmaking*, are both full of creative projects that everyone can try, whatever their level of skill. However, acquiring Bambi fired up my imagination. I was eager to seek out pastures new and to open myself up to fresh inspiration and experiences.

Travelling encourages creativity. You might see a familiar object in a different setting and find yourself thinking of unusual ways in which to use it. You might meet someone who shares their love of a local craft with you and decide to try it for yourself. Or you might come across a treasure that's way beyond your budget but that could be reproduced to some extent back at home. I hope this book will encourage you to think differently about what can be achieved.

Like lots of other people, I often go off the beaten track during my travels. I try and avoid the tourist hotspots and prefer instead to explore hidden places. I've always enjoyed rooting around in street markets and *brocantes* – French for second-hand markets – for unusual and inexpensive bits and pieces to take home. It's fun to hunt for thrifty little treasures – a fragrant bunch of lavender from a field in France, a delicately coloured crochet doily from a charity shop in Wales or a remnant of faded vintage fabric from an Italian street market. The trouble is that, once home, these items are often put away at the bottom of a drawer and soon get forgotten about. How much more satisfying to turn these personal mementos into something pretty or useful (or both) to remind you of happy times. That's when you need this book. Never again will you be stuck for something to make out of those postcards you didn't send, or the hand-worked tapestry you bought for a song.

But let's be honest: not every adventure can be turned into a handicraft. You'll also read about the ups and downs of life on the road, the melancholy that sometimes goes hand in hand with travelling solo, and the doubts about whether I could make it back in one piece. And there are things you definitely *shouldn't* try at home! The encounter with the elderly campsite Lothario, the near-death experience in the Gorges du Verdon, and a cautionary tale about taking your ageing camper van up over the Alps on a black ski run.

In this book you'll find suggestions for clothes, quirky souvenirs and upcycled home accessories, all reflecting the fascinating people I met, the beautiful places I visited and the interesting objects I unearthed during my travels. There are no-sew projects, as well as simple hand-stitch ideas and some that benefit from the use of a sewing machine. Turn to the back, and you'll find all of the 'makes' listed in order, with a key to tell you which ones are best constructed using a sewing machine (sm), which are best hand sewn (hs), and which require neither. Most of the projects here are relatively straightforward, but I've also included a couple more challenging ideas that require some prior knowledge of certain sewing terms. For instance, to make the Romantic Travelling Cape (p. 231) or the Sew on the Go Signature Top (p. 87), I'll guide you through drafting a simple pattern, while for the latter you'll also need to know how to attach bias binding. However, I've made a conscious decision not to include a 'sewing manual' with an explanation of sewing techniques and stitches, as I felt that doing so would change the nature of the book. So if you're unsure about what I mean by 'tacking', 'whip stitch', 'gathering' or 'hem allowance', then please ask a friend or relative, or refer to the many excellent resources available on the internet.

I suggest dipping your toe into one of the easier projects to start with and then, when you've built up your confidence, you can have a go at something more stretching. If you've never sewn before, I hope this book will inspire you to learn and find out more. Sewing is a life skill and we need to pass it on to the next generation.

This isn't necessarily the craft book I originally planned, nor the one you might expect, but creativity is like that – it doesn't always follow a straight line. Wrong turns are part of the process. So tear up the map and come and join me! Whether you're a crafter, a camper-van enthusiast or simply thinking about a change in direction, jump on board the Mobile Makery and see where it takes you. I hope this book will be your crafting companion.

Right, then. 'Are you sitting comfortably? Then we'll begin!'

1

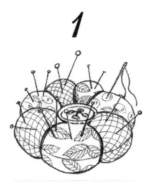

Your Essential Travelling Craft Kit

There are a few things that it's worth having in your craft kit if you're hoping to sew on the go. Obviously, it depends a little on your mode of transport. If you're backpacking or just taking a suitcase, then you'll need a scaled-down version. However, if you're lucky enough to have a camper van or caravan to travel in, then you can, hopefully, squeeze in all of these essentials!

- A selection of needles in different sizes including a large, blunt bodkin (this is great for threading elastic and can be useful for weaving too). Also include a couple of child-friendly plastic needles in your kit.
- A selection of different-coloured threads.
- A couple of balls of wool for weaving, making pom-poms, or even mending if you find a stray hole!

- A measuring tape – essential not only for sewing but also handy when you're visiting markets to check dimensions of objects you might want to buy.
- A ruler and a pencil – useful for drawing patterns.
- Pins – I like the ones with bobbly ends as they're easier to see.
- Scissors – really sharp dressmaking scissors, a pair for paper and a small, sharp pair for snipping threads, etc.
- A thimble – not everyone has one, but they're very useful, especially if you're sewing through thick fabrics.
- Safety pins in different sizes – always handy to have in your sewing kit, and great too in an emergency if you lose a button or your hem comes down.
- A seam-ripper – great for undoing your mistakes.
- Chalk or a fabric marker pen – either of these – essential for marking fabric. The special pen will fade in a matter of hours, so it doesn't leave a permanent mark.
- Elastic – a wider elastic (about 2.5 cm wide) is good for making garments; narrow elastic is also worth having in your kit as well.
- Buttons and beads – you can usually find really pretty ones on your travels, but have some in your kit to start with just in case.
- String – you never know when you might need it.
- Pom-pom makers in a couple of different sizes (see p. 192).
- Leather thong or lacing – great for making instant necklaces out of things you might find along the way (see p. 36)
- Ribbons, trims, pretty additions – I always like to have a shoebox full of things like this with me for when inspiration strikes.

- Fabric scraps – essential for patchwork.
- Old newspaper – useful for drafting patterns or making templates.
- Clear glue – not superglue! Something like UHU works well as a general adhesive.
- I'd suggest having an iron with you. It's a must-have for pressing seams as you're sewing, as well as being indispensable for the days you want to look well turned-out. Remember to take a travel adapter too, so you can use different sockets in different countries.
- A hand-crank sewing machine. I realise that this isn't going to be on everyone's list, but it does mean that you can speed-sew anywhere, whether there's electricity or not. I have a hand-crank sewing machine on board Bambi, and an electric machine at home. You can find some very good vintage hand-crank sewing machines on the internet for not too much money. They're great for learning to sew, as you're completely in control of the speed, and kids love them too.

Make a Patchwork Flower Pincushion

As part of your essential kit you should also include a pincushion, so you can keep all your needles and pins safe. We're going to start off with this lovely flower version, which can either be made from fabric you find during your trip, or from scraps of material that have real personal meaning for you. That way, however far you travel, you'll always have this comforting reminder of home close to hand.

Of all the textile crafts to try, I think patchwork is one of the best. It's perfect for a journey, as you can do a little bit every now and again to help yourself unwind. My hand-worked pincushion project is a gentle introduction to making. It's not difficult, and it fits in the palm of your hand, which gives it a lovely manageable quality.

Patchwork has a long and fascinating history, with different traditions relating to time and place. It was hugely popular during the 'make do and mend' era of the Second World War, when there was little money to spare and scant access to new materials. People had to reuse whatever they had. Today we should be more aware than ever about the amount of textile waste that's created, and patchwork is the ultimate upcycling project. Start with this small pincushion and you'll soon be moving on to something more ambitious. Try and work as neatly as you can using small stitches, matching the edges of each patch really carefully to get the best results. Also, think about the colours you use, and maybe place a dark pattern in the middle to give the flower a centre.

You'll need

- patchwork hexagon template (you can download this from the internet: I used the 2.5 cm or 1 inch size)
- scraps of fabric for the patchwork – cottons and crisp fabric work especially well
- scissors, needle (sharp and fine) and thread. You may also want to use a thimble

- finely cut fabric scraps (or even old laddered tights) for stuffing
- gold cord for edging (optional) and gold thread, if possible (any toning colour will do)
- a dab of glue

How to make

1. Trace and cut out your paper templates: you'll need seven for each side of the pincushion.
2. Put a paper hexagon in the middle of the wrong side of the fabric and cut out, leaving a 1 cm border all round. Turn the border inwards over the paper and tack the fabric in place round the edges. Press with your fingers as you go. Make all your patches in the same way.
3. To join the central patch to another patch, place right sides of the patches together. Knot your thread and slip the knot under the fold so it's hidden. Use a tiny whip stitch to sew the two patches together, picking up only the very edges of the fabric and trying not to go through the paper. Knot the thread at the end firmly. Now sew another patch into place to create a group of three. Continue until all seven patches are sewn together. Repeat for the other side.
4. Place your two 'flowers' with right sides together and whip stitch all the way around the edge, but leave a gap of two patches so that you can turn the pincushion right-side out. As you sew, pay special attention to the points and the corners, making sure they join together well.
5. Snip the tacking threads and remove all the paper patches. Turn the right way out, using your fingers to push out all

the edges, and a knitting needle or pen to gently reach into the corners.

6. Stuff the pincushion as much as you can with small fabric scraps, pushing them into the corners and sewing up the opening as you go. Leave a tiny hole if you're planning to add gold cord. If not, sew the whole pincushion shut. Either way, use your fingers to push the pincushion into as precise a shape as possible.

7. Take the gold cord and cut it to fit the edge of the pincushion (but add on a couple of centimetres extra). Put a tiny dab of glue on each end of the cord to stop it unravelling. Now stick the end of the cord into the tiny hole, stitch the cord around the edge by binding your thread over the top of the cord and picking up the edge of the fabric underneath with your needle. Trim any remaining cord and poke it back through the tiny hole. Sew up the remaining gap. You're done!

2

Straining at the Seams

You know the score. You're at your desk, idly scrolling through picture-perfect posts from total strangers, thinking for the millionth time about leaving the rat race behind: just you, your backpack and a rough plan on a piece of paper. On this dream journey there are no emails, no deadlines, no daily commute, no people vying for your attention or arguments with stressed-out colleagues. There's just the freedom of the open road stretching before you and a rendezvous with a crushed-ice cocktail at six o'clock. Then the phone rings, the bubble bursts and you get back to work with a sigh.

For many years I'd combined several very different jobs. While slogging my guts out working my way up the ladder as a BBC correspondent, I'd also decided to follow my passion for creativity and had trained as a professional hat maker. For a while I balanced shifts on the busy BBC news desk with working part-time for milliner-to-the-stars Stephen Jones. Then, just for good measure, I set up a mobile business running hatmaking hen parties too.

At one point, I devised and presented a series for BBC *Newsnight*. I travelled around the UK exchanging bed and breakfast for practical tasks like sewing and darning while investigating the return of the 'make do and mend' philosophy that coincided with the financial crash of 2007–8. During my six-week trip, which took me from London up to the north-east of Scotland and across to Glasgow, I interviewed numerous people, all disillusioned with the growth of consumerism. I met a struggling mum who was learning dressmaking in order to save money on her kids' new clothes, a Catholic monk who'd built his own hermitage and was living off the land, and a woman running craft nights in Edinburgh pubs. I patched jumpers, made curtains, gave free talks, and even fashioned a pair of trousers for a stilt-walker in order to literally 'make' my way around the country. At one point, I swapped a night in a hotel for one of my handmade hats. It got me thinking about how different our lives could be if we exchanged skills rather than cash in order to get by. I realised that in the UK we were becoming horribly lazy, reliant on others to do even the simplest of tasks and throwing things away rather than fixing them.

The journey for *Newsnight* was the inspiration behind my first book, *Chic on a Shoestring*, which was all about creating lovely clothes and accessories out of the sorts of things that people shove in the bin. I showed my readers how to magic a necklace from a pair of old shoelaces, fashion a pair of fingerless gloves from a worn-out jumper and make a fabulous vintage-style cocktail hat out of an empty cereal packet. The book did very well. It flew off the shelves in the UK, Australia and New Zealand, got snapped up by the US and was even translated into German (I'm *Fräulein Vintage* in Deutschland). A second book called *The Modern Girl's Guide to Hatmaking* soon followed, and before long I was writing a monthly column for a national magazine on how to live stylishly on slender means.

Around the same time I was asked to co-present a series on BBC Two called *Handmade Revolution*, helping amateur craftspeople hone their skills and up their commercial game. The winners got to sell their work in the famous Victoria & Albert Museum in London, the world's largest showcase of applied and decorative arts.

It was wonderful helping others to make the most of their talents, but I began to wonder what I was doing with my own. I started to feel I was spreading myself too thin. My various jobs just about kept me afloat financially, but there was little time to do anything other than work if I wanted to pay the bills on time. My personal life had suffered too. I was careering towards fifty and had no partner or children. In spite of my determination to follow my gut instinct and do something more creative, I'd got to the point where I was juggling too many different balls and felt in danger of dropping them all. I knew something needed to change, but I wasn't sure what. Deep down, I knew I was searching for a less complicated, less consumerist way of life, one where competition, career success and having the latest high-tech gadgets didn't matter. Ultimately, perhaps, I wanted to find my tribe, a community that shared similar values and a place where I felt I really fitted in.

Finding the Perfect Fit

Around this time my godfather died and unexpectedly left me a little bit of money. I immediately decided to spend part of this inheritance on a small camper van. I'd always dreamed of having a Mobile Makery, a stylish studio on wheels packed with all the equipment I needed to create beautiful things as I journeyed around the UK and perhaps even further afield. I'd never thought it would be possible, but due to his generosity, that fantasy was now partly within reach. I imagined myself exploring French *brocantes*, swimming in crystal-clear rivers and meeting a clutch of colourful creative characters while living in my wonderfully eccentric home on wheels. I'd have an old-fashioned hand-crank sewing machine on board so that I could sew wherever I fancied, and a mini gas hob to allow me to rustle up delicious meals made from simple fresh ingredients bought at local markets. In this dream, I'd support myself by selling my wares in sun-soaked markets and there'd be a sense of excitement whenever the Mobile Makery rolled into town – the local children clamouring to hop on board and make something! Of course, I'd love to have had a trendy split-screen VW or, even better, a quirky corrugated Citroën H van, but the first was too expensive and the second too heavy on the steering. So, a bit like Goldilocks when she found the perfect plate of porridge, I discovered a third van that was just right for me: a Bedford Bambi.

Now you've probably never heard of Bedford Bambis before. I hadn't either, until I saw one by chance parked up in a lay-by near Greenwich Park in London. Intrigued by the name and the small size, I'd asked the owner if I could take it for a spin and, amazingly, he'd agreed. Bambis (the company got permission to use the Bambi tag from Disney) are boxy little vehicles. At just under 2.5 m high and 30 cm shorter than a typical Ford Fiesta, they're creamy white in colour and, in all honesty, a little bit tinny. They're equipped with a petite 970 cc engine (not much more powerful than a large motorbike), but what they might lack in speed and style, they more than compensate for in price: Bambis usually retail for well under £5,000, making them one of the cheapest second-hand motorhomes on the market. They're also something of a rarity. While these British-built vans were the height of popularity in the eighties, only 1,500 ever left the production line, as one half of the company making them went bust in the early nineties. Bambi owners are, therefore, members of a very exclusive club.

The Bambi makes the perfect Wendy house on wheels. Inside, it's a bit of a Tardis: a two-berth van, the side benches were originally designed as single beds, although, I have to say, you don't get the most comfortable night's sleep on one of them, as they're very narrow. Much more luxurious is the double, created by slotting the tabletop and some boards down the middle between the benches. The seat pads are then assembled like a jigsaw to make a big rock-'n'-roll style mattress. Up above the driver's seat there's an extra space, which apparently is suitable for a young child to use as a kind of box-bed, but it's far too small. I can't imagine any child I know being happy to spend the night there, but it makes for decent extra storage. Then there's a tiny fridge, a two-ring gas hob, and a small sink with a tap. The original vans also came with a chemical toilet stored in one of the lockers underneath the benches. However, as using this contraption involved rearranging all the cushions, opening the locker, shutting the curtains and throwing any passengers out, many were removed.

It wasn't quite love at first sight, but I plumped for my own Bambi after only one date, having seen her advertised online by a garage in Southampton. I nipped down on the train to take a closer look and found a much-neglected van needing lots of TLC. How could I not pick her up, dust her down and give her a new lease of life? I (perhaps rather naively) bought her on the spot and proudly drove her back to south-east London, where I parked her on the street in front of my flat. It didn't matter to me that Bambi's top speed was 60 mph, that the interior electrics and fridge were broken or that I'd have to use a potty on board. Bambi would be my bolthole, my crafty retreat from the world.

Make Do and Mend

Whenever I had the spare time, I'd spend a few hours working on Bambi. I felt like I was building an escape pod outside my front door. First I papered her interior with the torn-out pages of a 1950s' dressmaking book and then started reupholstering the seats with a mixture of quirky vintage fabrics and souvenir tea towels. I changed the tatty blinds for floral curtains, added over-the-top bobble trim and spent many happy hours hunting down enamel mugs, retro kitchen equipment and crochet blankets to pretty up the space. The dream of having a personalised Mobile Makery kept me going through the dark winter nights and the long shifts working in the combative BBC newsroom.

Make a Souvenir Cushion Cover

You've probably bought a souvenir tea towel in the past or perhaps you've been sent one by a relative who's been on holiday. They often look fantastically retro, and as they're usually printed on fairly sturdy fabric, they make great cushion covers, as I discovered when I was doing up Bambi. Why not have a go at making one yourself?

This is nice and easy to sew, as it doesn't have a zip, just an overlapping envelope flap at the back into which you insert your pad. I've included instructions for a square-shaped cushion, but you could use the same method for any size pad. This is a sewing-machine project. See the photo in the colour plates.

You'll need

- a large tea towel
- a cushion pad (make sure your cushion pad is smaller than your tea towel)

- extra fabric, if necessary, for the back of the cushion
- dressmaker's chalk or fabric marker pen
- scissors
- thread, pins, sewing machine

How to make

1. Press your tea towel flat and decide which part of the design you'd like to use for the front of your cushion cover. Carefully measure and mark a square about 4 cm larger (all round) than your pad on the tea towel and cut out.

2. From the remaining part of the tea towel (or from some extra fabric) cut out two more pieces – one just over three quarters the size of the front (a), and the other half the size of the front (b). These two pieces will overlap and form the opening flap on the back of your cushion. Hem the two edges that will form the opening with a narrow hem.

3. With all right sides facing the fabric of the main square, place piece (b) on top of it, and then place piece (a) on top of that so that they overlap. Pin in place and machine stitch all the way around the square with a 1 cm hem allowance. Strengthen at the corners by reinforcing with a second line of stitching.

4. Trim the corners diagonally, turn the right way out, press, and slip your cushion pad inside. You're done!

My upcycling activities provoked mild amusement and a certain amount of cynicism among my neighbours, who loved nothing better than to stand and watch – and make unhelpful comments – as I revamped the van. But when I started découpaging Bambi's outside with posh wallpaper samples foraged months beforehand from a Brighton skip, they decided I'd completely lost the plot.

'That'll come straight off at the first sign of rain,' they sniggered. 'Who on earth would put wallpaper on the outside of a van? That rust bucket won't make it to the end of the road, let alone around Europe!'

To me, however, my decorating technique seemed perfectly rational. I didn't want a plain exterior, but I couldn't afford a state-of-the-art vinyl wrap, so why not just do it myself? I created a sort of patchwork effect, cutting out shapes from the wallpaper, sticking them onto the van with PVA glue and sealing them with several layers of clear outdoor varnish. It was extremely therapeutic playing with such a large canvas, making up the design as I went along. What's more, it worked. I had no garage and so Bambi stood outside on the street in all weathers, giving me a chance to test the exterior and see how it held up. As I'd hoped, the paper remained intact throughout several torrential downpours. Moreover, if the van's surface ever got scratched or damaged, I could just add more decoration as and when it needed repairing.

The exterior may have been sorted, but unfortunately, I still had no interior electricity. I'd been told by a camper-van expert that the wiring (the victim of a previous amateur botch job) was 'a death trap'. I couldn't afford the cost of getting it all redone and so I had the mains disconnected instead, which meant that, as the sink relied on an electric pump, I now had no running water as well as a redundant fridge and a potty for a toilet. I may have been travelling in a stylish van, but let's just say it was lacking in all mod cons.

The one thing I couldn't do without, however, was the means to cook, so I used the last bit of my budget to have the gas hob properly checked and the worn pipework replaced. There was no way I was driving anywhere without the ability to rustle up a fried breakfast or a pot of coffee. Even I had my limits.

In the course of just a few weeks my Bambi had been transformed from a plain Jane into a head-turning home on wheels. My neighbours were impressed enough with my handiwork to cease making jokes. Bambi and I were ready to hit the road.

Bambi Wins Them Over

Our first official engagement was the Bath Fashion Festival, where I ran a pop-up session making floral paper headdresses. Outside it was grey and dreary, bucketing down with rain, but inside Bambi remained perfectly dry and cosy, eliciting 'oohs' and 'aahs' from everyone who came on board. A couple of hatmaking parties followed for friends' kids who declared Bambi theirs and insisted on eating their birthday tea inside with the curtains shut. My little niece and nephew started asking after my van whenever I spoke to them on the phone. In their eyes, Bambi was a member of the family.

It soon became apparent that Bambi had real personality. She wasn't just a slice of self-indulgent escapism for me but the door to a creative world for others. Kids pointed and smiled when they saw her passing by and even the moody tearaway teenagers who lived a few doors down couldn't resist taking an appreciative peek inside whenever they thought I wasn't looking.

It was heart-warming to see what a positive effect Bambi was having on everyone around me, and I began to wonder if there was some way I could spread the love. Could I consider taking to the road for an extended period of time? How would it feel to leave everything behind to live and work in pint-sized Bambi for a few months on the trot? I couldn't even stand up straight in the van, for goodness' sake, so how on earth would I cope in such a tiny space? What about my job, my familiar home comforts and, more importantly, my friends? Fantasising about the nomadic life was one thing, but the reality might be quite another. I might feel rather lonely.

Would it be considered naive and foolish for a single woman nearing fifty to pack in her BBC salary for a precarious taste of freedom? Then there was the small matter of earning a living on the road. OK, I'd proved that Bambi was a great venue for workshops, but could I actually make enough to sustain myself and help fund the trip?

All these questions were running through my mind when suddenly the BBC announced a round of voluntary job losses. It seemed too good an opportunity to miss. Yes, I would be giving up an enviable career after many years of determined hard work, but

I wasn't happy. If I didn't do it now, then I would never summon up the courage. I applied for redundancy, and just a few weeks later found out that I'd been selected for the chop and would be leaving by the spring. It was no king's ransom, but enough to assuage at least some of my concerns. I seized my chance. The decision was made.

Spurred on, I found a lodger to rent my flat, got Bambi fully serviced, paid for European breakdown cover and even sourced a few spare parts, just in case I found myself stuck up a mountain far from home with a technical hitch. Armed with a map, my *Wild Swimming France* book, a satnav, a smartphone and a big box of my own handmade hats, I sketched out a rough itinerary for my journey. I would head to Belgium, then carry on through France and drive down to Italy. I'd see how I got on, then either continue further down south or drive back to the UK and journey up to the north of Scotland. I didn't want to over-plan. Having spent most of my career in an industry addicted to adrenaline and ruled by constant deadlines, I needed a break from it all. I wanted to give myself the opportunity to 'take the road less travelled' and leave behind the relentless negativity of twenty-four-hour news. I vowed not to look at the papers, scan stories on my phone, or tune into the radio for the duration of my trip. I would be self-sufficient, making do and mending my life as I went along, and perhaps even creating something new out of all the pieces I found.

3

A Maker's Journey

I set off from London on St George's Day, 23 April 2015. As Bambi eagerly revved up the ramp onto the Dover–Calais ferry I felt a tremendous sense of freedom. I thought of my colleagues back in the BBC newsroom in London, up against the clock as they tried to wrestle the latest story into submission. What a relief to leave it all behind.

Bambi was waved forward and tightly packed into the metal hull alongside dozens of other vehicles. I switched off the engine, locked the door, grabbed myself a coffee and found a cosy spot tucked behind a salt-encrusted window next to the canteen, where I could sit and watch the land slip gently away. From now on, it was just me and Bambi.

The boat was full of overexcited teenagers being chaperoned by tetchy teachers who'd drawn the short straw in the school-trip stakes. Outside on the deck, gangs of giggling girls stood huddled in groups while spotty schoolboy show-offs skidded past them on the sea-sprayed surface.

Watching them reminded me of my fourteen-year-old self, heading off to Normandy with my classmates. I'd never been to France before. As a family, we'd always spent holidays in Scotland, and so crossing the Channel on my own had felt like a real adventure. I still remember the outfit that I wore for my 'maiden voyage' – a matching jacket and trousers in mint-green glazed cotton that my mum and I had bought together.

Apart from my going-away outfit, my first trip abroad was memorable for two other reasons. First up, the Bayeux Tapestry. It was more than nine centuries old and over seventy metres long, and I could scarcely comprehend how meticulously it was made. I pictured each section being embroidered by a group of genteel, well-dressed women poring over the canvas, skilled and serious. I'd never come across communal craft on such an epic scale before, and I loved the fact that by forming a sewing circle the women had achieved something much grander than they could have done by themselves.

Secondly (and rather less high-mindedly), I spent nearly all of my carefully allotted French pocket money on a pair of white pedal-pushers. They seemed so exotic that even though they were slightly on the small side, I just had to have them. It was the first time that I'd had the opportunity to buy a piece of clothing independently. I splashed all my cash in one thrilling go and squeezed myself into the knee-length breeches. I've never forgotten the fabulous sensation of wearing something out of the ordinary, and I've been a sucker for cutting a (rather unusual) dash ever since.

Lille and the Storybook Garlands

This time round I bypassed Bayeux and headed instead for Lille, where I was starting my Mobile Makery adventure by staying with Melissa, a friend I'd known since childhood. Melissa and I share a passion for *brocantes*, and Lille has one of the biggest in Europe, the Grande Braderie, held on the first weekend of September every year. Much of the city centre gets cordoned off to make way for the hundreds of stalls and hordes of visitors all searching for that unique and elusive bargain. Melissa and I had already conquered the Grande Braderie on one of my previous jaunts, but just because I was visiting at a different time of the year, it didn't mean that we would have to forego our foraging fix. I knew that Melissa and I were bound to track down a second-hand sale of some sort. Nothing would keep us from our search for attractive tat and we would trawl the papers and online ads until we found a *vide-grenier*, the literal translation of which is an 'empty attic'. These events are held in towns and villages all over France, and a bit like the UK's car-boot sales, are a reliable source of desirable junk (and even antiques) at knockdown prices. Now that I was travelling in the Mobile Makery (which had so much more storage than the average car), I knew that I would be hard-pressed to resist vintage temptation.

Sure enough, just a couple of days after my arrival, we were off on our first mission with Melissa's three young daughters, Olivia, Josephine and Solveig, in tow. Over the years the girls had been successfully brainwashed into sharing our enthusiasm for vintage bargains and it didn't take much to bribe them into joining us. We set them the challenge of finding something special for €2 each, a mission they all accomplished with well-honed skill, picking out a pretty soapstone box, a necklace and a doll. I'd soon spent my own €2 (plus a little extra) on a pair of beautifully patterned floral curtains and a pile of quaint old children's books full of colourful illustrations.

Hints and tips for treasure hunting in flea markets and brocantes

- Although some markets are set up for contactless payments, most (especially smaller ones) still require the real thing. Make sure you go to a cash machine before you get to your destination, as you won't always find one where and when you need it most. It pays to have smaller denominations of notes with you too, as many traders won't have change. It also gives you the option of offering a smaller amount (and saying you have nothing more on you). A little white lie doesn't hurt when flea-market shopping! Keep your money in a safe place, preferably where it's not on show – a money belt that you strap to your body is a key travel item, in my opinion.

- It's a good idea to bring along a large shopping bag or, ideally, a hands-free rucksack so you have somewhere to stash your treasures when you snap them up.
- Be prepared to haggle and to walk away if necessary. If you don't speak the local language and you have a friend with you who does, then get them to do your bargaining for you. As soon as you reveal yourself to be a visitor, the price will probably go up.
- Be methodical. I generally like to do a walk-through of all the stalls first before I buy anything. If you don't, you might just miss a bargain, and you could also find a cheaper version of the same thing a few stalls down. That said, if you fall in love with something completely unique and special, don't hesitate to buy it if it's a good price. Chances are it might be gone when you get back!
- Flea markets are great sources of inspiration – an unusual vintage trim on a dress, or a cotton handkerchief with a striking floral print. Bring a notebook and pencil with you to jot down ideas and have your smartphone handy to take photos too. It's always best to ask if you want to photograph an item, as stallholders sometimes get annoyed if you take images without asking.
- Be aware that electrical items like lamps will need rewiring to make them safe for use. Grubby items will need to be washed as soon as possible, but don't discount something if it has a small stain. It might be worth the gamble!
- Lots of the projects in this book are based on items found in second-hand markets. Look out for things like: vintage

magazines and books about handicrafts (a good source of ideas and inspiration as well as being great for découpage); beautifully illustrated children's books; old-fashioned tea towels; crochet blankets; floral pillowcases; French linen bed sheets; French linen nightdresses (they can be dyed and turned into shirts); workwear; pretty vintage postcards (the older the better); old photographs; handcrafted trims that you can pick apart, learn from and recreate yourself; old hand-worked tapestries (you can always remove the frame if you want to use it for a project); embroidered tea-tray cloths; buckles and buttons, especially unusual and unique ones; curtains (great fabric and often very cheap); hat blocks (now very collectable); unusual jewellery; woven baskets (always useful and often beautifully made); sewing baskets (I just like them); enamelware (always adds a vintage touch to any kitchen) and pastel-coloured crochet doilies (they can be used in several different ways).

Thrilled with our haul and eager to host my inaugural workshop, Melissa invited a gang of friends and their offspring round to help us turn the books into stitched hanging paper decorations using my hand-crank sewing machine. Unfortunately we couldn't fit everyone into Bambi, and so we sat around Melissa's kitchen table instead, muddling along in a mixture of French, English and Italian. The children were delighted with the old-fashioned Singer, taking it in turns to wind the metal handle. Most of them had never had a go at sewing before, and it was wonderful to see their enthusiasm. Fuelled with home-made carrot cake and a glass or two of wine (for the grown-ups), it was a memorable way to start my journey. We might not have been stitching the Bayeux Tapestry, but it was communal creativity nonetheless.

Make a Storybook Garland

Making these garlands is the perfect project for teaching children how to sew, and a great way of repurposing old books, maps and music. They look lovely hanging up as decorations. This is a sewing-machine project. See the photo in the colour plates.

You'll need
- a large paper punch
- old books, maps or music
- thread, buttons or charms
- scissors
- sewing machine

How to make
1. Use a large paper punch (they're available online in all sorts of designs and sizes) to cut out a whole pile of shapes from your chosen paper and then just sew through them one

by one using the straight stitch on your sewing machine – make sure there's a little gap between each shape (the thread will automatically form a little chain) and enough thread left free at the top so you can hang your decoration when you're done.

2. Carry on sewing until you complete your garland. It can be as long as you like! You can tie something to the bottom too, like a little charm or a button.

3. You can also use these decorations as paper chains across a room.

4. If you make them using a small punch instead of a big one, you can wrap them around a present or hang them like tinsel on a Christmas tree (make sure you only use LED lights on your tree if you're hanging paper decorations on it).

One of my all-time favourite books is *The Artist's Way* by Julia Cameron, which was first published in 1992. It has helped redirect my creative compass many times. The author often talks about 'creative synchronicity', that moment when seemingly unrelated events come together to give particular resonance and meaning. So it was when Melissa took Bambi and me to visit nearby Roubaix and the Swimming Pool Museum. Back in the nineteenth century, Roubaix, which is twinned with Bradford in West Yorkshire, was a boomtown, its fortunes (like those of its English counterpart) closely linked to the prosperous local wool and weaving industries. The swimming pool was designed by architect Albert Baert and opened in 1932 to great public acclaim. It's a stunning example of the Art Deco style, but it wasn't only built to be beautiful, it was also a socially progressive space, a place where the workers could relax and get clean after their week's labours. The pool reflected the city's wealth and status, but when the textile industry fell into decline, so too did the pool, which closed in the early eighties.

Fortunately it was remodelled as an exhibition space and now houses a collection of figurative works from the nineteenth and twentieth centuries as well as paintings, ceramics, glass, furniture, jewellery and fashion. The Swimming Pool Museum is a reminder of Roubaix's affluent textile past as well as being a symbol of hope and cultural regeneration for a community that's beset with socio-economic challenges.

While the museum and its collections were definitely worth exploring, I was thrilled to find that our visit had serendipitously coincided with a temporary exhibition about the work of Parisian artist Nathalie Lété, one of my favourite contemporary designers. Her style has a unique quirkiness to it and I've often been drawn to her designs for brands like Anthropologie and H&M. Often naive, childlike and sometimes slightly dark, Lété plays with the ideas and images found in traditional fairy tales and seeks inspiration from her ever-growing collection of thrifted vintage paraphernalia and toys. She uses a wide range of craft techniques to express her vision:

drawing, embroidery, rug making, print and papier mâché, to name but a few.

For the previous few months the source of my own creative energy had felt depleted, but seeing her work, with its avalanche of colour and texture, was the equivalent of eating a delicious meal after being on rations. Exploring the museum shop afterwards, I discovered that Lété had curated a range of books and CDs, things that had acted as stimuli for her own artistic expression. It was like a generous chef passing on some of her favourite ingredients. Stumbling upon this exhibition seemed to me the perfect example of creative synchronicity at work. It felt like a clear sign that I was on the right track.

Antwerp Adventures

My next stop was Antwerp, a theoretically straightforward drive along the motorway. However, as I merrily made my way around the Lille ring road I suddenly saw a very low bridge ahead – so low, in fact, that I immediately had to slow right down in the middle of what was fairly fast-flowing traffic in case I took Bambi's roof off. In my panic I couldn't remember the height of the van and was forced to crawl underneath (much to the irritation of the impatient drivers around me) with just a couple of inches' clearance. Having congratulated myself on surviving intact, I then had to negotiate two or three more of these treacherous underpasses, each one more terrifyingly tight-fitting than the first. It should have been a warning to me that Bambi's unusual dimensions were going to lead to some interesting situations along the way.

Later that evening I was able to recall my first travel ordeal over a much-needed glass of wine with Iris, a Belgian friend that I'd first met through the BBC. Like me, Iris was also trying to balance the creative life with the more mundane. A talented blogger, she'd left journalism and had since made her mark by co-writing and photographing a bestselling cookery book with her sister. However, in spite of that success, she was still having to combine a number of different jobs to keep her head above water financially.

As luck would have it, I'd arrived just in time to celebrate 'food and fashion week', an annual event that shines a light on the creative quarter of Antwerp. Iris was busy photographing cool new bars and filing copy on glamorous launch parties. I happily accepted her invitation to tag along.

For those who've never been to Antwerp, let me fill you in. The city used to be the centre of the world diamond trade and now boasts a crazy mishmash of Gothic, Renaissance and Baroque buildings interwoven with Art Deco and ultra-modern architecture. This eclectic mix is also reflected in Antwerp's cultural scene, making it quite easily the coolest and quirkiest city in Belgium and possibly one of the most eccentric in Europe. Fashion is an essential part of the mix. Antwerp plays host to the wonderful ModeMuseum and is also home to the first-rate Royal Academy of Fine Arts, whose fashion department gave rise to the Antwerp Six: Walter Van Beirendonck, Ann Demeulemeester, Dries Van Noten, Dirk Van

SEW ON THE GO

Saene, Dirk Bikkembergs and Marina Yee. This gang really helped put Belgian fashion on the map. On graduating in the mid-eighties, they famously banded together to hire a truck for London Fashion Week, crossing the Channel with their latest collections stuffed in the back. They refused to accept no for an answer and, like me, took to the road in their quest to carve out a future for themselves.

This unorthodox spirit is still very much alive in a city where you often stumble upon unusual business combinations. Wasbar, for example, is a cool café-cum-launderette set up by two young entrepreneurs who've since opened several other outlets in Belgium. I've often wondered why more people don't launch launderette-based cafés, as they seem such perfect bedfellows. Who doesn't want a cuppa and a comfortable place to read while waiting for their washing to dry? Iris and I also visited Maurice's Coffee and Knits, the brainchild of Véronique Leysen, a former TV presenter-turned-knitwear designer. Inspired by her grandfather (the eponymous Maurice), she'd popped up in the former foyer of an old bank, turning a bland corporate venue into a splendidly offbeat series of snug little spaces. People could sip a coffee, stitch and bitch to their heart's content, and purchase one of Veronique's own unique designs if they were feeling flush. What an inspiration.

Tucked away in an attractive Antwerp suburb was another woman I very much wanted to meet during my trip. Babette makes the sort of vintage-inspired clothes that you can wear every day without feeling like you're living in the past, and I'd heard a lot about what a talented seamstress she was. Taught how to sew by her mother, Babette could remember falling asleep to the sound of the treadle-machine whirring away at home. Unlike many teenagers, who are eventually seduced by the lure of the high street and abandon their craft, she never lost the dressmaking bug and was soon making clothes for her friends. Apprenticeships with the likes of Dries Van Noten and Belgian milliner Elvis Pompilio could have seen her move into the world of haute couture. Instead she decided to set up her own bespoke dress label while working as a dental assistant to help bring in a steady income.

Babette lived on a rather imposing street full of Art Deco houses and after ringing the bell I stepped into a vestibule boasting a marble floor and a type of old-fashioned glass panelled cloakroom where, in days gone by, a porter might have sat reading a newspaper, waiting to relieve you of your fur coat. Numerous vintage handbags were stashed on the polished wooden hat stand, a brown alligator snap-fastening clutch, a smart Lucite shoulder bag and a richly embroidered pastel-coloured purse on a little gold chain. Babette's latest sewing project lay on a substantial wooden table by the window in the front room, and over a pot of violet tea she explained how she adapted old patterns to her own designs, adding unusual little details, like a contrast-coloured bow in a slither of designer fabric. Then she offered to give me a tour of her own wardrobe. It was packed with pretty handmade skirts and dresses in Babette's signature 1930s silhouette, all perfectly in keeping with her trim figure and neat, dark bob.

Sewing turned out to be just one of her many talents. When she wasn't working at the dental surgery or bringing up her two children (both of whom are now studying fashion themselves) Babette liked to indulge her passion for synchronised swimming. Her group, Solange's Travelling Wonder Show, performs in Art Deco pools across Belgium, and she even designs and makes the retro-style swimwear that they all wear for their gala performances. Before I knew it, I'd commissioned my own perfectly fitting frock, complete with decorative trim made from a remnant of fabric bought at the Dries Van Noten textile sale (apparently he has one sale a year and it's well worth knowing about).

Five years after that first tête-à-tête, Babette and I are still firm friends. I've made hats for her shows, and I'm now the proud owner of a second bespoke Babette number – this time an elegant black evening dress made in exchange for a holiday in my London flat. It's always worth exploring creative swaps like this in order to help make a slender budget go further.

4

Back in Brussels

A few years ago I was posted to Brussels to work as a foreign correspondent and producer for the BBC. The job was very exciting but also stressful, and during the two years I was based there I travelled extensively throughout Europe, covering everything from terrorist atrocities to natural disasters. In fact, my first week in the job saw me board a plane for Switzerland at eleven o'clock at night, equipped with nothing more than a map of the country ripped from the in-flight magazine. On arrival I picked up a hire car and drove on my own through the night to report on a tunnel fire in which several British people had died. It was all par for the course. My colleagues and I were never really off duty so there was little chance to completely relax and get to know Brussels properly.

Whenever I did have some precious spare time, I'd head to the characterful Marolles neighbourhood and its focal point, the Place du Jeu de Balle flea market. At first sight the market looked like a dumping ground for piles of unwanted junk displayed on tatty old blankets, but I soon discovered there were countless treasures to be unearthed there. I bought everything imaginable at that place, from a beautiful gilded mirror almost as tall as me to a pair of fifties cat's-eye sunglasses. You could have furnished an entire house from top to bottom with unique pieces from this one market alone.

I'd often imagined returning to Brussels in a more laid-back frame of mind, free from the constant need to monitor my mobile phone 24/7, but never in my wildest dreams had it occurred to me that one day I might trundle through the officious EU quarter in a wallpaper-covered van.

The contrast with my former life couldn't have been more stark. Impeccably dressed Eurocrats stared in frank astonishment at Bambi as she stopped at traffic lights and navigated her way past the smart chauffeur-driven cars. They no doubt dismissed me as a hippy dropout, and it made me smile to think that just a few years previously I'd been one of them too. Now I was on my way to Jeu de Balle to meet Jacqueline Lecarme, a little-known artist who makes sculptures out of reclaimed plastic. Jacqueline shuns the limelight, and I suppose that's how I'd managed to live in Brussels for so long without knowing anything about her.

If ever you're lucky enough to mount the dimly lit creaking staircase to her studio, you'll find a *brocanteur*'s dream. The cupboards of her vast, high-ceilinged workroom are laden with overflowing boxes of retro belt buckles, hair combs mounted on old advertising display cards, and drawers of multicoloured buttons. There are numerous shelves stuffed with shoehorns and shaving brushes, hair rollers and pens, in fact anything and everything made from plastics. She has a magpie's eye for gaudy treasures, not only scouring markets herself but also speaking to antique dealers for leads to deadstock from old warehouses, where boxes of untouched items often lie abandoned for years.

Galalith (like Bakelite, but made of milk protein) is Jacqueline's favourite medium, but it's getting harder to find, so she's always on the lookout for other options. She assembles all of these disparate elements together to create fantastical animal statues, human masks and unique pieces of jewellery. Even the most basic sculpture needs at least thirty separate plastic components and requires hours of painstaking and intricate work. As far as I could see, Jacqueline designed instinctively. There wasn't a computer in sight. She made straight from her imagination, fastening random pieces together one by one to realise the composed form that existed inside her head.

I couldn't believe how a talent like Jacqueline's had gone under the radar for so long. Her wonderful creations, the accumulated work of so many years, were simply piled up high on every surface, so that everywhere you turned there was something unexpected. I recognised a certain obsessive quality about her work that I'm also aware of in myself. She simply *had* to do what she had to do, even though it didn't bring her much financial reward. Her natural shyness and her lack of PR know-how meant that she hadn't received the recognition she deserved. It's so difficult for artists today. Not only do they have to be outstanding at what they do, they also have to be social-media savvy. Perhaps in the past you could have quietly got by doing your own thing, supported by a generous patron. Nowadays, with less money around, it's those who are seen and heard that attract investors. Fortunately, over the last few years, Jacqueline has at least had some exposure through a creative collaboration with Walter Van Beirendonck, who has featured her stunning accessories on the catwalk. Nonetheless, meeting Jacqueline was a timely reminder of how and why so many artists and craftspeople slog away unrecognised for years, never reaping the rewards they so richly deserve.

I couldn't ever make anything as beautiful as Jacqueline's pieces, but seeing her collection of bric-a-brac got me thinking about a simple project using the vintage-plastic belt buckles I'd collected over the years. Their graphic shapes and mid-century colours make such a statement, and they're usually only a couple of quid each.

Make a Vintage Buckle Necklace

Use a leather thong or piece of coloured string to thread up an old-style buckle or two to create a unique and stylish necklace. Remove the metal prong carefully first with a pair of pliers. If you're feeling adventurous you can use a jewellery drill to make a hole that will allow you to attach a chain instead. If you do use a drill, make sure you follow the manufacturer's instructions, wear goggles, and use a clamp to keep your buckle stable as you work. See photos in the colour section.

When I was originally planning my journey in the Mobile Makery, I was determined to try and put on an event in the Place du Jeu de Balle in honour of all the happy hours I'd spent there. I knew that it wouldn't be easy to cut through the red tape. After several unsuccessful emails in Franglais to council officials, trying to explain what I wanted to do, I finally got in touch with a friend of a friend who, at the time, ran a gorgeous shop called La Frénésie right next to the flea market. Not only did Caroline Moreau sell beautifully selected fresh flowers and foliage, she also curated a collection of affordable homewares from the fifties, sixties and seventies. Striking and eclectic, her shop was packed with everything you never knew you wanted.

Caroline was completely on my wavelength and kindly sought permission for me to park Bambi in the cobbled square outside her front window so that I could run a pop-up workshop there.

On a sunny Saturday morning, supported by a gang of former colleagues and thronged by curious kids, I put on my first outdoor craft event of the journey. In return for a couple of euros per person, everyone got to make themselves a decorated paper badge from the colourful second-hand picture books I'd picked up so far on my travels. One of my visitors, a little Iraqi boy with the most charming smile, was dropped off by his father and stayed for about three hours. He scarcely spoke any French (or English), but his lack of language skills didn't matter. He made badge after badge, and then sat inside Bambi on the patchwork seat, completely absorbed in an encyclopaedia about British native trees (luckily it had escaped being cut up and made into something else). I think he'd quite happily have lived in Bambi for ever.

Make a Paper Badge

These badges are really easy to make and can be worn by children and grown-ups alike! See the photo in the colour plates.

You'll need
- a paper punch
- old books, magazines, etc.
- an empty cereal packet
- glue
- glitter
- ribbon

- a safety pin
- scissors
- a sticky label or strip of paper

How to make

1. Use a large paper punch to cut out a special image from a book, then punch a second matching shape from an old cereal packet.
2. Stick the paper image to the printed side of the cereal packet, then dab glue around the edges, dipping into a shallow dish of glitter.
3. Allow to dry, then cut out 20 cm of ribbon, halve it, and fold over a safety pin.
4. Stick the ribbon to the back of the badge and glue a strip of paper or put a sticky label over the ribbon to hold the safety pin in place.
5. Decorate your badge with additional trims if you desire.

Bambi and I were kindly hosted during our stay in Brussels by another former BBC friend, an Irishwoman with flaming red hair who'd met her Belgian architect husband while waiting in a cinema queue one fateful night. She'd since swapped the media for motherhood and now had two gorgeous small boys, Finn and Lorcan, to look after. I loved being submerged in the chaos of family life. The kitchen table was like a battle zone. Torn-off pieces of baguette scattered the surface like bullets from a gun; plastic soldiers smeared with strawberry jam lay submerged in mountains of half-used plates and cups. The boys seemed to be everywhere, jumping off sofas, skidding across parquet floors and bumping down staircases. After the orderly confines of Bambi, where everything had to be kept in its allotted place, this riot of noise and colour was just what I needed. It felt life-affirming.

Ailsa and I laughed at just how much things had changed. Only a few years before we'd led fairly 'glamorous' lives working for the foreign news desk. Now here we were, Ailsa running around picking up small pairs of discarded pants and me living in a van and putting on badge-making workshops at the flea market!

When I lived in Brussels, I rented a lovely flat with high ceilings and ornate cornicing on the sophisticated Place du Châtelain in the Ixelles area of the city. Nearby, on Rue de la Page, was a beautiful little boutique that enticed me in on a regular basis due to its mix of antiques and unique finds. One day I popped inside to have a browse wearing an unusual fifties' black-and-white cotton frock that a very special aunt had passed down to me. The dress was covered in a print that's best described as 'fantasy handwriting' and it immediately caught the eye of Dorothée, the charming woman standing behind the counter. Before long the two of us were laughing away as if we'd been friends for years.

It transpired that Dorothée was a costume maker and as I got to know her better, I became increasingly fascinated by her job, which often involved sourcing vintage pieces to create a specific look for a production. I'd sometimes join Dorothée in her hunt for the perfect brocade waistcoat or lace cravat. We'd rake through the Jeu de Balle, picking up numerous other little trinkets along the way, and then install ourselves on a sunny terrace nearby for a restorative cup of coffee and croissant. I eventually admitted to her that I was beginning to feel out of kilter in my own job. I'd dreamed of becoming a BBC foreign news correspondent, but now that goal was truly within reach, I'd started to have doubts. I wasn't hard-skinned enough. I began to dread the phone ringing, bringing details of another catastrophic event that involved dropping everything and getting on a plane. I started to experience occasional panic attacks and wondered how I would cope if I was sent to a hostile environment or war zone, something that was expected of you if you wanted to be taken seriously. Dorothée was very supportive when, after another year or so, I made the momentous decision to quit my Brussels job and return to London to enrol on a hatmaking course at the Kensington and Chelsea College. I'll never forget my boss's shocked expression when I announced that I was leaving my highly sought-after position to study millinery. Little did I know that a few years down the line Dorothée would follow in my footsteps and become a hatmaker herself.

During my Mobile Makery trip to Belgium I had a call from Dorothée telling me she'd heard on the grapevine that a local milliner was retiring and closing her long-established business. Mireille Van Dem Boine was selling all her stock, including a very rare, traditional flower-making press and all the equipment that went with it. Dorothée, who by this stage was already making her own stunning hand-dyed silk corsages, was interested in having a look, and wondered if I wanted to come along too.

It was another example of creative synchronicity at work and an opportunity that I couldn't resist. To find an entire milliner's workshop up for sale is a real rarity and something I doubt I shall ever see again. Imagine a dusty basement crammed with flower-making supplies dating back at least seventy years: bundles of paper stamens in every colour and size, rolls of fine green silk velvet for fashioning leaves, feathers from myriad species of bird, and delicate spotted lace veiling of a quality you'll no longer find today. As well as this treasure trove of delights was the solid iron antique flower press and all the petal-punching tools that went with it. Dorothée and I were both breathless with excitement, and before we'd even had a chance to examine the stock in detail, Dorothée had decided that she was going to purchase the whole lot. Mireille was over the moon to find not only a buyer, but someone who would treat her lifetime's collection with passion and respect.

5

Paris in Bloom

It was while we were chatting to Mireille that I came up with the idea of taking Dorothée to Paris to visit one of the world's leading faux-flower makers, the house of Legeron. Founded in 1880, Legeron creates handmade blooms for couture clients such as Chanel, Dior and Givenchy. I'd been there before while studying millinery and I knew that Dorothée would love to explore behind the scenes of this historic place.

I phoned ahead and explained that my friend had recently bought a wealth of flower-making tools and was keen to learn as much as she could about this historic craft. We were welcomed with open arms and invited to come the following day. Call me a coward, but I wasn't willing to navigate the traffic chaos that is the French capital in Bambi, so instead I tucked her up safely on a friend's driveway in Brussels and Dorothée and I caught the train.

Legeron oozes mystique from the moment you step inside the elegant, tiled entrance hall of the genteel old building on Rue des Petits-Champs. You wind your way up a circular wooden stairwell that smells of wax polish to a door with an understated nameplate and an old-fashioned brass bell. Once admitted to the inner sanctum, you're led into a showroom full of antique mahogany cabinets where exotic blooms made from every conceivable material lie nestled in layers of rustling tissue paper stashed in hundreds of glass-fronted wooden drawers.

But the real treat is to see behind the scenes. We were shown the secret leather-bound ledgers that contain the recipes for tinting and dyeing petals a particular shade; precious sketchbooks full of hat designs from the fifties and sixties, complete with swatches of fabric; the room where swathes of silk are stretched on wooden frames and stiffened with gelatine before being stamped into shape; then the workshop itself, where a dozen or so *petits mains* (the dexterous craftspeople) sit perched on stools forming flowers in intricate detail, using tools that are more than a hundred years old. It's heartening to think that in today's trend-obsessed world, where fast fashion is the norm, there are still pockets of people prepared to put in the hours to make beautiful handmade treasures – collectable heirlooms displaying traditional skills that are still being passed on from generation to generation today.

Dorothée was awestruck by her visit to the Legeron atelier, scribbling ideas and sketches into her notebook as fast as she could. My challenge was to come up with a straightforward project that captured the essence of the handmade but used simple techniques.

My answer? These pretty blossom hairpins. Sprinkle your coiffure with a smattering of these flowers and you'll soon have a skip in your step, whether you're in Paris, New York or Rome.

Make Spring Flower Hairpins

I first saw a version of these blossom-like flowers on a silky vintage nightdress case that I bought at a French flea market. I unpicked them stitch by stitch to see how they were made. This is my own interpretation using cotton organdie – a crisp fabric that's easy to dye and manipulate. Go on, give these a whirl. They're not difficult. This is couture craft for a fraction of the price. Not quite what you'll find in Legeron, but still *très belle*! See the photo in the colour plates.

You'll need

- cotton organdie fabric in cream or white
- scissors
- felt-tip pens
- small paintbrush and some water
- needle and thread
- extra yellow thread for stamens
- a glue gun
- large, old-fashioned hairpins
- a scrap of felt

How to make

1. Cut the cotton organdie into strips 40 cm long and 5 cm wide. Each strip makes one flower. Fold in half lengthways then add some colour on one side with the felt-tip pens. Blend and bleed the colours together with the paintbrush and a little water.

2. Once the fabric is dry, thread your needle with a double thread and put a knot at the end. Work a small running stitch along the raw edge of the folded strip for 5–6 cm, then make a large stitch up to the top and down again to form a V.

3. Now pull up your stitching. As you pull the stitches together, you'll see that they gather the fabric into a petal shape. Repeat the previous step to create another petal, and so on until the end of the strip.

4. Once you get to the end, you should have made a few petals.

5. Arrange the petals in a circle and stitch through the middle to form a flower shape.

6. To make stamens, form a loop by wrapping yellow thread round your first two fingers a few times. Take off and tie in the middle.

7. Sew the yellow thread to the centre of the flower and, when secure, cut the loops of the thread.

8. Use the glue gun to stick the flower to a hairpin. Cover the join on the back by gluing a small felt circle over it. Scrunch the flower a little so it's not too perfect. You're done!

Hidden Gems

Paris is full of secret ateliers fashioning everything from leather bags to musical instruments. If you're on your own millinery mission you should definitely arrange a rendezvous with Lorenzo Ré, who owns La Forme. Lorenzo originally trained as a sculptor in Italy but then moved to Paris, where he started making wooden hat blocks, the moulds that milliners use to give their materials body and form. Perhaps he reasoned that producing blocks might be a more straightforward way of earning an income. It seems to me that artists often have to make compromises and split themselves in two, focusing on the work that creates a profit in order to support their more experimental and personal pieces, only made if time allows. When I visited Lorenzo, he was adding the final details to a troupe of handmade puppets, their heads all lined up on a high shelf waiting to be varnished. Each one displayed such expressive detail that you could read the character and personality straight away. The figures reminded me of the stone gargoyles that a mason might have sculpted on the arch of an ancient cathedral to ward off evil spirits.

Hat blocks come in a huge variety of shapes and were once produced in their thousands. The generic domed versions called crown blocks, which correspond to different-sized heads (just like shoe lasts), are the most easily recognisable and were considered the workhorses of the industry. The milliner places the crown block on a stand then stretches, manipulates and pins a base of stiffened felt or straw over it using steam. The material can be tweaked to achieve different effects. The brim is often made separately, but in a similar way on a larger, much flatter block. The two pieces are left to dry and are then carefully cut off and stitched together to create a whole. The hat is finished inside with a petersham ribbon to help it keep its shape, and is finally beautifully trimmed. It's a long and skilled process and explains why buying a handmade couture hat can sometimes be rather expensive.

The hat blocks that Lorenzo makes are in a different league altogether to the domed variety you might find in your local antique shop. His sculpting skills are sought out by fashion houses such as Dior, Givenchy and Chanel as well as illustrious designers like Philip Treacy, probably the most famous milliner in the world. Looking around Lorenzo's studio, you'll get a tantalising glimpse of what's coming next on the catwalk, and the walls are plastered with photos of the unusual and sometimes outlandish styles you might see at Royal Ascot. But while Lorenzo's hat shapes end up gracing the pages of *Vogue*, they start out fairly humbly as pieces of soft wood being worked by a craftsman with simple tools like a lathe and chisel in a workshop full of sawdust and the scent of fresh wood shavings. Lorenzo's only guide is a sketch on a piece of paper, or if he's lucky, a rough shape that's been suggested in something like papier mâché. Each block he creates is a miniature work of art. He's been toiling away alone in his workshop, a stone's throw from La Bourse, since 1962 with his wife acting as his admin assistant. Back in the sixties the neighbourhood was alive with the sound of hammering, sawing and sanding. Now Lorenzo is just one of a handful of hat-block makers left in the whole of Europe. A dying breed. Few want to take on this solitary craft, which brings relatively little monetary reward.

Not far from La Forme is a shop called Ultramod, which has come straight from the pages of a haberdashery history book. It's been open for more than a century, and stepping over the threshold is like time-travelling. There are actually two shops to see. On one side of the street you'll find a huge variety of hats designed by the in-house team, as well as all manner of millinery materials and an astonishing selection of ribbon in a rainbow of colours. In the boutique opposite there's a vast array of traditional upholstery trims, tassels, cording and other sewing notions, all beautifully displayed in the original drapery cabinets. Much of the stock was bought from French factories that were forcibly closed down during the Second World War, so what's on offer is one of a kind.

For many people, Paris is all about the sights. Those famous monuments, the museums, and perhaps a romantic stroll along the Seine or the Champs-Elysées as the spring flowers burst into bloom. But for me, Paris's charm also lies in its plethora of second-hand markets, arguably some of the best in the world. You can always find the unexpected and unusual, and while it's harder to find bargains nowadays, it pays to be persistent. One of my best buys, admittedly about twenty years ago now, was a bagful of vintage wooden hat blocks just like the ones I saw in Lorenzo Ré's workshop. I was on my way to catch the Eurostar back to the UK, heading to a Métro station through a street market, when I spotted a pile of them in a cardboard box underneath a table. They were ridiculously cheap, costing about €15 each, whereas these days new ones will set you back anything from £100 upwards. I wish I'd bought them all, but I couldn't pack more than four into my already bulging rucksack.

To be honest, even if you don't purchase anything after perusing the second-hand delights of the French capital, you'll still come away brimming with ideas. As I mentioned before, it helps to take photos so that you can refer back to the things that caught your eye when you get home: a ravishing piece of lace on a tattered dress, bright fabric buttons or a romantically faded silk flower. Just soak up the atmosphere and tuck yourself onto a corner terrace with a *café au lait* to make notes, daydream and watch passers-by.

I can't resist sharing my tips for two of Paris's best weekend flea-market finds here. Check before you visit for the latest opening hours.

- St Ouen/Clignancourt (Métro Garibaldi). It's vast and can be touristy, but it's still worth going for the incredible variety of unusual objects for sale. Be selective, and if you're short on time then check out the Daniel et Lili shop in the covered Marché Dauphine and the other stalls in the Marché Vernaison.

- Porte de Vanves is an outdoor flea market with more of a neighbourhood feel. You'll still see stallholders playing an amicable game of chess, and stopping for a glass of wine and a stump of saucisson at lunchtime.

Nobody can get a true taste of Paris without making food a priority, so as well as spending time sampling the gastronomic delights cooked up by others, I decided to have a go myself and learn a skill I could take back home. You see, much as I love the famous La Durée for its delicious pastel-tinted *macarons* and fancy packaging, I can't really justify the expense. So I decided on a thrifty alternative instead, and joined a macaron-making workshop at La Cuisine, a little cookery school just minutes away from Notre-Dame. The lesson was in English so that I and the other ex-pat students didn't struggle to understand the recipes, and thank goodness for that, as there was quite a lot of complicated technique to take on board!

We first learned the difference between French and Italian meringue and then had a go at making both. I think we were all rather nervous to start with but, fortunately, baking with others always helps create a bond and soon we were laughing at our attempts to beat the mixture into the perfect stiff peak and daringly hold the bowls over our heads. My favourite part, though, had to be the tinting. A couple of drops of red, green or violet food colouring are all that you need to create the chalky, muted tones that high-class *macarons* are noted for – but it's all too easy to end up with a garish green or ruddy rose. Shading the meringue was like being a watercolour artist and reminded me of the skilled artisans working at the Legeron atelier, painstakingly fashioning delicate life-like petals from pieces of plain silk.

Soon our piped pastel-coloured discs were being shovelled by the trayful into the ovens and we settled back to drink tea (very British) and chat as the kitchen filled with the warm scent of baking almonds. The excitement mounted as our first efforts emerged – did they exhibit the required 'foot' and the little 'frill' so evocative of these sweet treats? We were all ridiculously pleased with the results – they all seemed very professional to us! We sandwiched them together with home-made strawberry jam as well as chocolate-, pistachio- and lemon-flavoured buttercreams, also made by our own fair hands. I was astonished. They looked and tasted just as good as their expensive shop-bought counterparts, and I was thrilled that, once back home, I'd have the confidence to make them again and complete the picture by packaging them up in beribboned boxes – a home-made gift inspired by my trip. Learning to make something yourself, be it jam, chutney, or *macarons*, is such a lovely thing to do. Not only do you gain a life skill, but you have at your fingertips a means of saving money and giving enormous pleasure at the same time.

Continuing my culinary adventure, I also visited the kitchenalia mecca that is E. Dehillerin on Rue Coquillière. A temple to the craft of cookery, this shop is almost 200 years old and was a favourite of culinary legend Julia Child. It's the main Parisian haunt of both home cooks and Michelin-starred chefs alike, and no matter your level of skill, you'll likely find some sort of fascinating gadget that you've never clapped eyes on before. I spent a good hour perusing the shelves of one section groaning with gleaming tins for a variety of French *pâtisserie*, including tarte Tatin, brioche, madeleines and croquembouche. Next door there were tottering towers of funnels, ranging from those that looked big enough to pour petrol into a tractor to the teeniest fairy thimble size. Drawers opened to reveal expensive professional sushi knives. Giant preserving pans were stacked alongside stockpots and copper fish kettles while ornate glass jars displayed myriad skewers, tweezers and bundles of butchers' string. As a memento of this magical place I bought a very simple plastic scraper that boasted the name of the shop in metallic green lettering along one side. It's designed to help you remove dough from the kitchen surface after kneading your bread. A simple implement, but the best €2 I've ever spent and a reminder of Paris each time I bake a loaf.

Full of fresh inspiration, Dorothée and I waved goodbye to Paris and returned to Brussels, where I planned to pick up Bambi and set out on the next part of my trip. It was getting on for the end of May, the weather was just beginning to improve, and I was keen to test my ability to travel and live in the van full time. It had been lovely retracing my former footsteps and catching up with old friends, but the open road beckoned. I stuck a pin in the map and headed for Reims, the unofficial capital of the Champagne region. It seemed fitting to celebrate the start of my solo trip with a glass of bubbly in the spiritual home of fizz!

6

Striking Out Alone

One of the many marvellous things about France is that it boasts a comprehensive network of official temporary stopovers designed specifically for camper vans, or 'camping cars', as the French call them. They're often run by the local council or *mairie* and most places, from small towns and villages right through to large cities, have at least one set aside for holiday makers. Called *aires de services* or *aires de stationnement*, they're not the same as campsites, as they offer only the most basic of facilities. Usually there'll be a freshwater tap to fill up your container, a waste-disposal point and sometimes an electric hook-up. Very occasionally you'll find a loo on site too, but if you're travelling in a camper van like Bambi with no on-board facilities (except for your handy vintage-style floral china potty) you soon become adept at tracking down the nearest public WC anyway. The best thing about the *aires* is that they're either completely free or cost just a few euros per night, so they provide budget travellers with an extremely affordable way of seeing the country.

Before leaving the UK I'd bought myself an official guide called *Les Aires de Service Camping-Car*, an invaluable little book that became a kind of bible for me. As a single female traveller, I was slightly nervous about the prospect of sleeping overnight in Bambi, but I realised that if I wanted to save money, I'd need to pitch up in the *aires* as often as I could.

It was a fresh, blue and spring-like afternoon and Bambi soon settled comfortably into her stride on the motorway out of Brussels. It's not a particularly long drive to Reims, but I stopped to stock up with essentials at a supermarket en route so that by the time I reached the outskirts of the city it was getting on for six o'clock in the evening. I keyed the address of the *aire de service* into my satnav, but on arrival I couldn't get in. It seemed to be blocked by some kind of barrier. Was it full? Was it closed for repairs? It was already too late to search for a proper campsite, and given that the tourist season hadn't started, I guessed that most places wouldn't yet be open for business. I had to find somewhere to stay, but my pride prevented me from booking into a hotel. This was meant to be my first real taste of life on the road so I could hardly go and get a room. What would that say about my sense of adventure? No, I'd test my resilience by parking up in the city and simply stay the night in the van there. It felt like a rite of passage, something I had to do in order to claim my credentials as a proper traveller. So I turned around and went in search of a potential side street.

I drove around for a bit trying to find the right place, but the residential suburbs seemed eerily quiet in the gloaming. Before leaving Brussels, my friends had lectured me about taking care of myself and had thrown in a couple of scare stories about overnight camper-van attacks for good measure. With their dire warnings ringing in my ears, I headed for the city centre, where I imagined I might feel safer with more people around. I followed signs for Reims cathedral and parked up right next to it, in the glow of a street lamp. Bambi must have looked rather out of place in the cathedral close, but I felt sheltered there under the watchful gaze of the stern stone angels. I made myself something to eat in the semi-darkness, nervously looking out of the window every few minutes expecting to see the *gendarmerie* arrive with blue lights flashing. In fact, my only visitor was a rather dapper-looking gentleman taking his portly French bulldog for a walk. He stopped and stared at Bambi, and I waved back through the window in what I hoped was a way that expressed carefree nonchalance. He looked puzzled, and I suddenly realised that I might have been mistaken for some sort of mobile moll. Mortified, I opened the back door and stuck my head out, explaining that the camper-van park was shut, and that I'd decided to stay by the cathedral for the night, as I felt more secure there. He seemed somewhat bemused by my rather odd account (probably putting it down to English eccentricity), then gave me a hesitant thumbs-up and quickly scurried off home. Heaven only knows what he really made of me.

I retreated, deciding that it might be a bit too much to actually put on my pyjamas and make up the bed, so instead I stretched out fully clothed on one of Bambi's side benches. Not the most comfortable start to my trip – and I hadn't even had the chance to sip my celebratory glass of fizz!

Although it was now almost mid-May, it was still pretty chilly once the sun went down, and that, coupled with my nervousness at being parked up randomly overnight, meant that I slept fitfully, imagining every voice and approaching footstep to be a threat. As it got light, I saw that I had parked in a pay-and-display zone, so I dutifully went and bought myself a ticket from the machine. Hardly the rebel traveller!

Once the cafés started waking up for the day, I went in search of a reviving coffee and gave myself a good talking to. From now on, I would have to set certain ground rules if I wanted to avoid parking in city centres alone at night. I would make sure I arrived in places well before dark and I'd locate the *aire* with plenty of time on my hands, just in case I had to make a plan B. My new code of conduct confirmed, and my appetite sated, I set off for my next port of call, a small town called Joinville just two hours' drive away.

On paper, Joinville wasn't anything special, but it looked like a good option for a quick pit stop. Joinville boasted a basic *aire* in a well-appointed spot down by the river alongside a clutch of sleepy canal boats. It cost just a handful of euros, had free Wi-Fi and the few houses scattered nearby kept a wary eye on things.

Walking into the centre, I discovered that the river narrowed and continued to meander into the town, running under old stone bridges and carving a sparkling path through rather quaint streets.

It was the sort of quiet, unassuming little town that, had you grown up there, you'd feel desperate to leave. Then, a few years down the line, you'd realise it was actually rather beautiful and return to set up home with your own children.

That first night in Joinville I slept for twelve hours solid, wrapped up under a duvet with a cosy hot-water bottle to stave off the cold. I felt cocooned in my little Bambi, soothed to sleep by a curiously comforting frogs' chorus resonating in gentle waves from the reed beds. It was the perfect relaxation sound loop.

The next morning, I found a friendly café where I could surreptitiously get washed and clean my teeth, order a croissant and charge my laptop. It was exactly the idyllic resting spot I needed to take stock and gather my thoughts. I went on lazy walks, wrote my blog, and slowly started to unwind, preparing simple meals in the van and eating them at the riverside picnic table from where I could watch the barges glide by. I realised how mentally drained I was and relished the chance to simply 'be'.

Occasionally other vans bowled up and the owners would sometimes pop over for a chat, attracted by Bambi's unusual good looks. No matter what nationality the occupants, they were all fascinated by my camper. One of the visitors was an elderly French gentleman who'd brought his severely disabled daughter out for a short touring holiday. He'd lost his wife the previous year and had a photo of her taped to the windscreen so that she was never far away. I really felt for him, being left alone with the huge responsibility of looking after his daughter. The travelling life brings you into contact with people taking refuge from all sorts of personal challenges.

Next to the camper-van stop was a hair salon and as I found myself chalking up my fifth day in Joinville (so much for the quick visit), I realised that it might be a good idea to make an appointment. While I was managing to keep fairly fragrant (thanks to the facilities in the local café and a good supply of baby wipes), I missed having freshly washed hair. Having it shampooed professionally felt like the height of luxury after almost a week of roughing it, and I relished the sensation of the running hot water on my scalp and the accompanying sensual head massage. As I sat there, luxuriating in the reclining leather chair, I noticed that they sold decorative feathers designed for creating hippy-chic tresses. I'd never seen them before, and on the spur of the moment I asked to have a few woven in. Washed, cut, blow-dried and with a flash of coloured feathers to boot, my new 'do' signalled the start of my life as a nomad. Bambi and I now matched. We were both colourful, curious and slightly offbeat.

It felt deliciously reckless watching other people set off for work in suits while I brewed a pot of hot coffee in the van. I wondered how long I could live like this, and how it would feel to make this my 'normal'. Sitting outside in the sun, I spread the pages of the road atlas out in front of me and hatched a plan to head for the north of Italy via friends in Bourg-Saint-Maurice on the French–Italian border. We'd have to see how things went after that. There was no pressure to clock up hundreds of miles for the sake of it. And so, with that in mind, Bambi and I set off for the beautiful fortified town of Langres in the Haute-Marne region, a good-looking place to stay for a couple of nights.

Langres

According to *Reader's Digest*, Langres is one of the fifty most beautiful towns in France. Built around an ancient hilltop fortress with historic ramparts, some parts date back 2,000 years. It looked ripe for exploration, and so I booked into a proper campsite just inside the city walls. It was a joy to have running water again. There's something about a shower when you haven't had one for days that seems like an utter indulgence. That first evening, feeling completely scrubbed and clean for the first time in a while, I walked round the seven gates and twelve towers of the ramparts, taking in the stunning, far-reaching views, then strolled into the centre to find a little restaurant to eat at.

On the way, I passed an interesting-looking shop selling all sorts of upcycled goodies, including a variety of accessories made from old hand-worked tapestries and needlepoint canvases. I've amassed many of these during my travels. They're such beautiful objects in their own right and are a real tribute to the skill and patience of the maker. What better way of showing them off than by turning them into wearable art – and that's where this simple bag comes in.

Make a Tapestry Book Bag

Remember that tapestries can be rather thick, so take care when you're sewing, and use a strong machine needle. Be prepared to turn to hand stitching if the going gets really tough. This is presented as a sewing-machine project, but you could also make this bag entirely by hand if you wanted to. I'd suggest using a strong backstitch and a double thread if you do. See the photo in the colour plates.

You'll need

- a vintage tapestry around the size you want for your bag
- lightweight iron-on interfacing for the back of the tapestry
- an iron
- measuring tape, ruler and fabric-marking pen (or chalk)
- fabric for the lining, the back of the bag and the shoulder strap. (If you don't have a long piece of fabric for the strap. you can always join two pieces together.)
- sewing machine, scissors, pins, needle and thread

How to make

1. Press the back of your tapestry flat. Cut out a piece of iron-on interfacing the same size and iron to the back using the manufacturer's instructions. This will stop the tapestry fraying when you cut it.

2. Using a ruler and fabric pen, mark out your bag on the back of the tapestry, leaving a 1.5 cm seam allowance all the way round. If you're not sure what shape to make your bag, base it on a large book or an A4 piece of paper. Cut out.

3. Now, using this as your pattern, cut out another three pieces of fabric exactly the same size. Also cut out a shoulder strap 10 cm wide and a comfortable length for your body (plus extra at the ends for seams).

4. Pin the tapestry to the backing fabric (right sides together) and machine the bottom and sides together. Reinforce the corners with an extra line of stitching. Remove pins, trim the corners diagonally, turn the right way out and press with an iron.

5. Now for the lining. Pin your two pieces of lining fabric together (right sides facing) and stitch round the sides and along the bottom. Remove pins, trim the corners diagonally, turn the right way out and press with an iron.

6. Fold the strap fabric in half with right sides together and stitch down the length to form a tube. Turn the right way out (use a knitting needle to help you to push it through) and press.

7. To assemble, fold over the top of the bag, then pin your strap into position onto the bag at the corners. Take care not to twist the strap. Tack in place and remove pins.

8. Slip the lining into the bag itself (wrong sides of the lining facing the inside of the bag). Fold over the top of the lining so it sits neatly inside the bag just below the folded edge. Pin in place, tack, then machine stitch all the way round. Repeat for strength. Remove any tacking stitches and press again. It's a portable piece of art!

The following morning I got chatting to a Frenchwoman who'd parked up next to Bambi. She revealed that her husband had died just a few months previously. During their long marriage, they'd done everything together, and his death had come as a complete shock. In order to try to force herself to be more independent, she'd found herself a little dog and invested in a compact motorhome. She was on her way south to meet up with relatives for a short stay, and the two-day journey was giving her much-needed practice at travelling alone. I wasn't the only one test-driving a solo camper-van life. I really admired her determination to branch out.

It was now almost the beginning of June and with the weather beginning to warm up a little, I was eager to dive into the pages of my *Wild Swimming France* book. This publication, brimming with tantalising colour images of the most beautiful lakes and rivers in which to take a dip, had been one of my main escapist reads back in London. I'd sit on my sofa looking out at the drizzle and the dreary brick terraces, imagining how it would feel to take the plunge in a pristine natural pool in the middle of rural France.

Wild swims have always been part of my life. As children, my brothers and I would spend two weeks every summer up on the north-east coast of Scotland in my mother's home town, Montrose. Running headlong into the stinging chill of the North

Sea or plunging into the peaty embrace of the glacial River Esk was always one of the highlights, as was the promise of a 'chittery-bite' or a sweet treat afterwards. However, despite growing to love the satisfying afterglow of cold water, I'd always fancied swimming outside in a milder climate and ticking this off my to-do list had been part of the plan for my journey.

Leafing through the pages of my book over breakfast in Langres, I came across a tempting entry for the Jura region. 'This is waterfall country,' said the writer, 'where great rivers gush from underground caves and quiet lakes for peaceful swimming lie hidden within rolling hills.' It sounded idyllic. A wild swim in the Jura had to be my next goal.

A Miniature Home on Wheels

I chose Camping Lac de Narlay near Lac d'Ilay to stop at after discovering it quite by chance following a conversation with a lady in a car park after I took a wrong turn! Described in the book as 'a perfect lake with grassy shores and shallow water to ease you in', the campsite was a lovely laid-back place, an alternative hippy haven not far from the Swiss border. It was basic but beguiling with abundant green slopes where you could park up freely and even build an open fire if you wanted to. Down a little track nearby was a tiny bakery selling fresh bread and on site was a small bar serving drinks and snacks.

The sun was beginning to give out some real heat during the day, and so I felt inclined to stay, spending the inside of a week swimming, reading, sewing and cooking up delicious meals from fresh ingredients. I got chatting to a lovely Swiss couple who'd pitched their tent nearby. Both mid-career teachers with grown-up children, they were enjoying spending some quality time together and exuded an easy, relaxed affection for one another that was heart-warming to be around. They invited me to join them for dinner one night and we ended up sitting out under the stars talking animatedly about life's simple pleasures and how important they are for our mental well-being. I also shared an aperitif with a group of French forty-somethings, all friends who lived nearby, but who fancied camping to get away from the day-to-day demands of their kids and families. We laughed a lot together, all of us crammed inside Bambi raising a glass of wine to life's adventures – both great and small.

The common theme at this campsite was the pared-back lifestyle, and because of that, it drew the sort of people who didn't need very much to feel content. A roof (or canvas) over your head, sunshine, clean water to swim in, simple, tasty food and friends to toast it with. I felt I fitted in here and that I was meeting 'my kind of people'. Although I'd brought a lot of crafting paraphernalia with me, I was actually travelling fairly light in terms of my day-to-day necessities. I was just like a snail with her cosy home on her back.

Bambi was certainly proving to be the perfect pint-sized bolthole. By night, she resembled an intricately decorated child's jewellery box containing all their prized (but not very expensive) possessions. I'd lie there, the interior lit with dozens of sparkling fairy lights, listening to the sound of guitars gently strumming in the dark. By day, I'd improvise an al fresco dining area, hanging my home-made brocante bunting in the trees and filling my little picnic table with jugs of wildflowers picked from the surrounding hedgerows. Being able to express myself through Bambi was bringing me real pleasure and it was wonderful to see how, yet again, the van was proving a delight to others. It was incredible how quickly strangers became travelling companions as we spent a few hours in each other's company.

Make Brocante Bunting

What is it about bunting? It immediately conjures up a party atmosphere. While in Brussels I'd even seen street bunting made from old football shirts, something I'd never have thought of repurposing so imaginatively! I fashion bunting from all sorts of things, including old wallpaper, fabric remnants, zips and ribbons.

This bunting is made from the crochet doilies that once adorned the dressing tables of the middle classes all over Europe, setting off their china figurines to perfection. Painstakingly created, in a variety of pretty pastel colours, these doilies are no longer in vogue and you'll therefore find them in second-hand shops everywhere. Have a go at making some of my brocante bunting yourself and celebrate the handiwork of these wonderful women crafters, whose labours often went unnoticed. This is a sewing-machine project. See illustration at the start of Chapter 7.

You'll need

- a selection of crochet doilies
- an iron
- a long length of woven tape (or ribbon) at least 3 cm wide (the length depends on how long you want your bunting to be)
- thread to match your tape
- sewing machine, scissors, pins

How to make

1. Sort your doilies. Small ones can be sewn onto the tape whole; larger doilies need to be cut in half. Press them with the iron so they're nice and flat.

2. Press a fold along the length of your tape with the iron (this will make it easier to slot your doilies into place). Lay it on the floor and position all the doilies you wish to use for your bunting inside the fold. (I like to place everything at random, so no measuring is required). Make sure you leave a good length of tape at each end so you can tie it up. Pin each doily in place.

3. Stitch in one continuous straight line along the tape, ensuring you catch everything in place as you sew. Remove the pins one by one as you work your way along. Tie your bunting up and let the party begin!

I hoped to reach my friends in Bourg-Saint-Maurice by the second week of June, and I still had a few days in hand before getting there. I toyed briefly with the possibility of visiting Lyon, France's historical silk-weaving centre. I'd lived there for two years while working for the TV broadcaster Euronews during the late 1990s, but I realised that a diversion there would take up too much time. And so instead I typed Lake Annecy in the Haute-Savoie into the satnav. It lay about halfway along the route to my friends' place and should have been perfectly manageable in a couple of hours. Unfortunately, the satnav got it wrong. It failed to take into account the numerous twists and turns, as well as the gruelling ups and downs of the route up towards the mountains.

I had a feeling that the hard drive would take its toll on Bambi and I was right. After being on the road solidly for some three hours, I was trundling down a steep hill into a small village when I hit the brakes. Nothing happened. I could smell burning rubber and a sound like air escaping from a balloon. I pulled on the handbrake immediately, feeling pretty shaken, scared about what might have happened if I'd been travelling at speed. I pulled over to let the engine and brakes cool down for a while, trying to decide what I should do for the best. I was in the middle of nowhere, it would be dark in a couple of hours and I had little option other than to gingerly carry on and try and find somewhere to stay. So, nervously, I started Bambi up again. The brakes seemed OK, but nonetheless I crept extremely cautiously all the rest of the way to Annecy, wondering how and where I could get the van checked over.

I arrived rather exhausted and stressed just as night fell at Camping du Lac in Talloires-Montmin. It wasn't where I'd originally planned to go, but I was keen to let the van rest completely, and simply chose the first decent-looking place I found and headed there. I was very lucky. With simply stunning sunsets and a breathtaking view over the water from Bambi's back door, I was allotted a prime spot for under €20 a night.

The next day the campsite owner, Jean-François Marie, came over to check whether I was all right. I'd explained my predicament on arrival to the lady at reception, and Jean-François wanted to see if he could help with the name of a local garage. He told me that he'd completely fallen in love with my little van and was curious to know more about my journey. I offered him a glass of wine, and soon we were chatting away like old friends. He promptly bought two of my handmade hats, and then over lunch presented me with a wonderful magazine from the early 1900s, full of colour plates of paintings by famous French artists. A former top-level skier, and a huge sailing enthusiast, he'd invested in the campsite after being forced to cut down on his sporting activities after a couple of major health scares. It was clear that he was a thoroughly sociable man, full of *joie de vivre* – the perfect host.

Hearing of my passion for all things vintage, Jean-François suggested I caught the bus into Annecy itself to take a look around. Often nicknamed the Venice of the Alps due to the amount of water surrounding it, back in the nineteenth century the city was known for its linen and cotton goods, as well as glass, cutlery and earthenware products. Strolling the streets I came across a little antiques shop that sold lots of beautiful table linen. Hanging in the window were dozens of hand-crocheted lace doilies that looked just like snowflakes. I was fascinated to learn how they'd been stiffened into decorations. The shop owner told me that her secret was sugar starch, a method traditionally employed by the Elizabethans to give structure to their fancy lace ruffs. It worked a treat until they ventured out in the rain! Have a go yourself – it really does work. If you find little tiny doilies, they'll be perfect for hanging on the Christmas tree!

Make Sugar-Starch Doilies

You'll need twice the amount of sugar to water (i.e., two cups of sugar to one cup of water). Heat slowly in a pan to make sure all the sugar has dissolved. Allow to cool.

Dip your doilies into the solution, squeeze out the excess and lay flat on a board covered with cling film or a plain plastic bag. Allow to dry overnight. Tie with ribbon to hang.

You can also make a decorative crochet container by

covering a small bowl with cling film and using it as a mould. Put the sugar-dipped doily over the bowl and allow to dry overnight. Remove the mould in the morning. Perfect for serving chocolates or sweets!

After three nights in Annecy, it was time to hit the road once more. Unfortunately, Jean-François' garage hadn't been able to see Bambi in time, and so I called ahead to my friend Sam in Bourg-Saint-Maurice to explain that I would need to get the van checked out while staying with her and her French husband, Paul. I knew it was a bit of a risk driving the couple of hours to Sam's, but having done a circuit of the lake, I felt fairly confident that the brakes had only malfunctioned because of the heat and the strain of the day's drive. I also knew that although my French was reasonably good, I wasn't quite up to going into a garage on my own and discussing a plethora of tricky technical issues. It would be much better to have Sam or Paul on hand to translate.

Black Ski Run

I hadn't seen Sam for many years, although we'd stayed in touch sporadically since I'd left Euronews, where we'd first met. I'd been a guest at her wedding, a romantic and memorable affair held in her husband's home town, where the two of them had lived ever since. Like many local men, Paul worked in the mountains during the winter helping prepare the slopes for the ski season, while in the summer he undertook a range of building projects. He and Sam lived on land that housed a few different generations of his family. It's not always easy to live side by side with one's in-laws, but Sam had done fantastically well at practising domestic diplomacy.

Paul had constructed their home pretty much single-handedly. It boasted a magnificent panorama of the Alps from the first-floor veranda and was full of rustic detail, with a big open hearth, sturdy floorboards and lots of generous wooden beams, giving the space the feel of a chic chalet. It retained the comforting smell of woodsmoke, even on a warm day when the fire remained unlit.

Just a few kilometres away in a tiny hamlet, Paul was helping a friend renovate another place, a secret hilltop hideaway. It would have done Heidi proud. Perched on the side of the mountain, it had vertiginous views down into the valley below and was full of snug corners where you could tuck yourself away with a thick wool blanket and a mug of cocoa. In the field behind, a horse cropped the grass, taking its stunning location completely in its stride.

Seeing these self-build houses and unique renovation projects made me realise just how unfortunate it is that practical subjects are so rarely taught in schools any more. Many of us don't know how to darn a sock, change a plug or fix a leaking tap ourselves, let alone build a house from scratch. Here in the mountains it felt different; hands-on skills were truly valued and still passed on from generation to generation – through pride, as well as necessity. When you're living a long way from the electrician or the plumber, it's vital to be able to DIY (Do It Yourself) and it saves you money too.

I remember being shocked a few years ago while putting on a collage workshop for children at Charleston, the former Sussex home of Vanessa Bell and Duncan Grant, members of the Bloomsbury Group. The idea was to create a mixed-media composition of the house and grounds using scraps of fabric, textured paper, yarn and natural finds like twigs, seed-heads and leaves gathered from the gardens. The children were all provided with a square of hessian on a wooden frame and encouraged to stitch their finds into place using wool and large needles. Of the twenty or so youngsters who took part, only two or three knew how to hold a needle, let alone thread it or actually sew anything. Most of my time was spent showing the children how to tie a knot to prevent the wool slipping straight through the canvas and out the other side.

In an era of fast fashion, some people are completely oblivious to the time and effort it takes to actually create something from scratch, and we've become correspondingly wasteful too. Mass consumerism and large-scale manufacturing (often to the detriment of the workforce and the environment) have been responsible for the disconnect between an item and its worth. Learning how to sew gave me an early appreciation of the value of things. I'm more respectful of garments I've sewn myself, as I know how much love and care I've put into making them. I'm more likely to mend them and much less inclined to get rid of them, which is better for the planet too. According to the charitable social business Clothes Aid, 350,000 tonnes (or around £140 million worth) of used but still wearable clothing goes to landfill in the UK every year. That's a shocking amount. If you can sew on a missing button, fix a zip or let down a hem, you're doing right by the environment and saving yourself money too.

Paul had grown up in a family that knew all about making and mending. His ancestors had owned a local mill called Arpin that specialised in weaving cloth from the fleeces of the sheep that graze in the four surrounding valleys. The mill was founded in 1817 on the banks of the Versoyen River, which provided glacial water to wash the wool as well as power to drive the generators when electricity came to the area. Arpin's most famous product is known as Drap de Bonneval, which was worn by some of the first high-mountain guides. Later the same fabric clothed the Italian expedition to the Himalayas, and in 1949 was adopted by the French Polar team, led by the famous explorer Paul-Émile Victor. Today the company's still going strong and continues to weave some of its textiles on a collection of historic looms that have now been given special protection under French law.

I was keen to come up with a simple upcycled project inspired by the woollen mill and the mountains and had a go at designing a hot-water-bottle cover made from one of the many old jumpers Paul had stashed away. My basic rubber hot-water bottle had kept out the overnight chill in the van, but I rather fancied a softer, more tactile cover. This seemed to fit the bill perfectly and is a wonderful way of repurposing your own worn-out sweaters.

Make an Upcycled Hot-water-bottle Cover

Everybody needs a hot-water bottle. Imagine a chilly night without one! Pop your hottie inside a cover made from an old jumper, and not only will you keep the heat in, but you'll be doing your bit for recycling too. You can even make use of jumpers with holes in them, as you can sew a pretty decoration or patch over the top of any hole. Make-do and mend at its best. This is presented as a sewing-machine project, but you could sew it by hand if you wished. See the photo in the colour plates.

You'll need
- a hot-water bottle
- an old roll-neck jumper (you'll need a tight-ish roll neck for this to work properly)
- sewing machine, scissors, pins, needle and thread
- felt/buttons/scraps of fabric for decoration

How to make
1. Turn your jumper inside out and insert the hot-water bottle up through the jumper so the neck of the bottle fits snugly inside the roll-neck.

2. Pin around the hot-water bottle to get the right shape and then ease it out through the neck.

3. Trim back the jumper to leave a seam allowance of 2 cm all the way round, then tack and remove pins.

4. Machine stitch (using either a zigzag or a straight stitch) around the tacking line, then repeat for strength. Remove the tacking and trim back excess, leaving a small seam allowance. Zigzag stitch again to stop any fraying.

5. Cut out a decoration from felt or fabric and hand sew onto the front of the cover (or to cover any holes).

After having spent the last few weeks on the road, it felt very luxurious to be sleeping in a proper bed with an en-suite bathroom. In return for board and lodging, I offered to help Sam restore her Fiat camper van, Morris, who was long overdue a bit of a makeover. We got to work sewing cute curtains out of a bundle of Ikea fabric and updating the table with a slick of sticky-backed plastic. While we were busy pottering around making things, I dropped Bambi off at the local garage to be thoroughly checked out for any lingering brake problems. I certainly didn't fancy driving on into Italy over the Alps without being sure that everything was working properly. I couldn't help but laugh at the celebrity reception Bambi received, with the mechanics falling over each other to have their photos taken posing at the wheel. If only I'd charged for each snapshot, I'd have covered the cost of the work and the change of brake fluid!

Over the Alps

As the crow flies, Bourg-Saint-Maurice is only a few miles from the Italian border, but there are two alternative ways of reaching it. Most heavy traffic takes the long way round via the Mont Blanc Tunnel, but there's a much more direct route if you're up for it. The Col du Petit Saint-Bernard, or Little St Bernard Pass, features in the hair-raising opening scenes of the film *The Italian Job*. Just south of Mont Blanc, it's more than 2,000 metres above sea level, and during the winter it's essentially a daredevil black ski run, closed to all traffic. Come June, however, the road opens up again (weather permitting) and anyone who fancies a challenge can give it a go and enjoy the breathtaking views and the technical driving. There's a sharp ascent of around 25 km to the top followed by a dramatic descent into the Aosta Valley below. It would be quite a feat for most drivers, but especially for the owner of a heavily laden thirty-year-old van that's had a recent glitch with its brakes. I don't quite know how, but somewhere along the line, I got talked into it, and a couple of days later, Paul offered to accompany me up to the border along with his dog Cannelle, who's the same size as a St Bernard, the famous rescue dogs that originate from these parts.

It was early summer in the valley, but as we climbed, the air quickly cooled. I could feel the addition of Cannelle's huge weight in the back of the van and switched down into the lowest gear as Bambi valiantly crawled up the sharp incline, taking the tight bends slowly, one by one. About an hour or so later, it started to get incredibly misty, but Bambi pressed on, gritting her teeth and grinding steadily up through the pass towards the frontier. I was so focused on the road that I scarcely looked around me, but the fog meant I would have seen very little of my surroundings anyway – a real shame, as the scenery is meant to be jaw-dropping. It seemed to take an age to reach the top, but eventually I saw the WELCOME TO ITALY sign looming out at me through the grey drizzle. Reaching the summit was a heady moment – I swear that Cannelle barked in delight!

We parked Bambi up in a lay-by to let the dog out for a run as Paul and I stretched our legs. It felt quite surreal. It really was still winter up there, and soon we were having a snowball fight alongside a bunch of crazy VW fans on their way back from a rally on the Italian side of the pass. I was bare-legged and wearing a light dress that I'd put on in the relatively summery climes of Bourg-Saint-Maurice, and so to warm up we dived into the Bar Ristorante Du Lac and ordered a café latte. I could scarcely believe I'd made it. Only seven weeks earlier I'd set off across the English Channel with Bambi, never imagining that I'd find myself sipping proper Italian coffee 2,000 metres above sea level with Mont Blanc on the doorstep.

Rather belatedly, it dawned on me that Paul and Cannelle were stuck up at the border with no transport back. I apologised profusely. Perhaps they could hitch a lift? How could I have neglected to ask them how they were going to get home? But it appeared that I had nothing to worry about. Paul gave me a huge hug and flashed me a bright smile. 'Don't you worry,' he said, 'Cannelle and I are walking back. We know the way!' And with a friendly wave this marvellous mountain man bade me *adieu* and he and his canine companion strode off, disappearing into the fog with complete confidence. Apparently, they were safely back home long before Bambi and I had made it down the other side.

What followed was a white-knuckle ride around innumerable hairpin bends. I hit the brakes continually but, much to my relief, they seemed to be working fine and there was no telltale smell of burning rubber this time. The weather remained dire and so I glimpsed little through the windscreen apart from the road ahead, but it didn't matter, I was just over the moon to have guided Bambi safely over the Alps.

Suddenly I saw road signs and place names in Italian, there were no croissants or baguettes in the bakery windows, and even in this bilingual buffer zone you could tell that you were no longer in France. When you travel by road or sea rather than by plane, you notice all the subtle and nuanced changes that come with crossing frontiers – the shift in accent, the smell of the cigarettes, the clothes that the children wear and the taste of the ice cream. An overland journey provides a wonderful opportunity to celebrate the rich diversity that we're lucky enough to have on our doorstep.

Bambi and I were bound for a campsite in Aosta, which is about seventy miles north-west of Turin and the capital of the valley in which I found myself. I planned to stay there for a short while to get my bearings and brush up on my language skills. I've always loved everything about Italy – the art, the music, the food, the wine and the people. I do speak a little Italian (although it's not a patch on my French), but I've always found that enthusiasm and goodwill go a pretty long way when trying to make yourself understood.

When I lived in Lyon, I shared a flat with an incredibly handsome Italian man with whom I was madly in love. I once went to visit him in Palermo, hoping that perhaps I might be in with a chance after hearing that he'd split up from his previous girlfriend. I vividly remember strolling with him through his local piazza one balmy evening, walking his dog. Suddenly a flurry of barking strays appeared from out of nowhere, making a beeline for us. We were soon trapped by a barrage of baying hounds, and he had to hoist the whimpering animal high above his head to keep it from being mauled. It seems the dog was as attractive to the local canine population as Pepe was with the ladies. Regrettably though, I was put firmly in the friend zone, so I didn't make any progress with him. My knowledge of *la bella lingua*, however, came on by leaps and bounds.

With Bambi safely ensconced in the campsite, a rather sanitised sort of a place with little character, I decided to treat myself to a night out to celebrate my safe arrival. There was a decent-looking trattoria nearby and so I had a shower, dolled myself up and went in search of my table for one. The warm, convivial atmosphere soon put me at ease, so I asked for a menu and browsed the tantalising

Upcycling Bambi with wallpaper samples
found in a Brighton skip

Detail of Bambi's wallpapered exterior

Bambi detail

The interior of Bambi before work begins

Bambi's upcycled interior with seats covered in a variety of vintage tea towels & floral fabrics

Bambi's new look

Heading to France on the ferry

Sewing kit essentials

Your essential sewing kit should include some sharp scissors

The Patchwork Pincushion

The Souvenir Cushion Cover

A fascinating visit to Jacqueline Lecarme's Brussels studio where she creates sculptures from vintage plastics

Brussels – The Gold Thimble

The first workshop of the journey making Story Book Garlands in Lille

Storybook Garlands

The famous fleamarket in Brussels

La Frénésie in Brussels

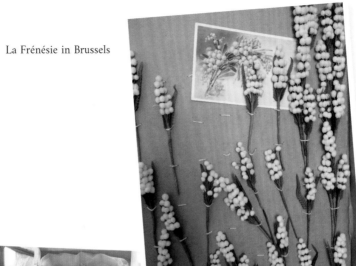

Beautiful fleamarket finds

Vintage buckles: you can remove the metal prong with pliers

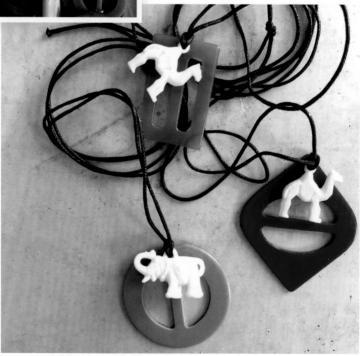

Vintage Buckle Necklaces with added mini charms

The Paper Badge can
be decorated in any
way you like

A selection of paper badges being made

The finished Spring Flower Hairpins

Vintage doilies inspire in so
many ways – pictured here
with Spring Flower Hairpins in
the making

Vintage millinery braids

Buckets of wildflowers decorate the picnic table

Tapestry Book Bags

Tapestries are lovely just as they are, or you can turn them into bags and cushions

Bambi parked up in the shadow of
Notre Dame cathedral in Reims

The pretty French town of Joinville

Lake Annecy

An al fresco picnic

The cosy Upcycled Hot-Water Bottle Cover made from an old jumper

At my hand crank sewing machine in Bourg St Maurice making new covers for my friend Sam's campervan

list of northern Italian wines – Nebbiolo, Barbera, Valpolicella – the names rolled off the tongue like rich velvet. I ordered myself a glass of Barolo (delicious) and then perused the pizzas, wood-fired and available in every conceivable flavour. Ah, the wonders of Italy! I chose all my favourite toppings – tomato sauce, Parma ham, spicy salami, mozzarella, mushrooms and artichokes. It was going to be quite a feast. I called the waiter over to ask for some chilli oil and a few shavings of Parmesan cheese. He seemed friendly and personable, and feeling rather sad at leaving my friends behind in Bourg-Saint-Maurice, I relished the chance to have a chat and practise the language. Now, I'll admit to being overly optimistic when it comes to Italian men, assuming them all to be passionate, effusive, a little cheeky, but essentially chivalrous. The waiter returned with the Parmesan and grated it over my pizza.

'You remind me of my former American girlfriend,' he said. I smiled in anticipation of a charming compliment. 'Tall, blonde... big boobs.'

My smile faltered. Not the most promising start to my Italian adventure. It didn't exactly bode well.

A Little Lost

'Hello, I'm reading your blog,' shouted the man in the van next to mine as he rolled down the window, waved his iPad at me and pointed to the web address emblazoned on Bambi's door. 'It's very girly, isn't it?'

I laughed. It hadn't dawned on me that my blog content might be construed as 'girly'. 'I'm Stan,' he grinned. 'I'm here on holiday with my wife, Lily.'

In fact, Stan and Lily were part of a gang of friends who'd come to Italy to celebrate their fiftieth wedding anniversaries. Refusing to settle for a knees-up down the road at their local pub, Stan and Lily, along with Colin, Val, Ken and Clare, had driven all the way from the Lake District in a couple of very swish motorhomes the size of buses. I was impressed. They were in Aosta because it's prime mountain-biking territory, and this lot, in spite of being in their seventies, were all bike mad.

That evening the weather took a turn for the worse and it started bucketing down with rain. Maybe I was just missing Sam and Paul, but for the first time since leaving home I felt a real pang of loneliness. My map of Europe stretched out before me like an endless piece of string. Bambi felt a bit chilly and miserable in the rain – even with the fairy lights on – and I cursed the lack of heating. I was contemplating switching on the gas hob for a bit of warmth (I know, it's a VERY BAD thing to do) when there was a knock at the door. Stan wondered if I wanted to join them for a drink. Their van, the bigger of the two, was decked out with luxury adjustable seats, ample leg room, a dining-room table, a shower cubicle and a fully functioning kitchen. How could I refuse? After a few bottles of wine, we were all getting on famously. They insisted on modelling my stash of hats, which caused much hilarity. Sadly no sales, but I felt a little cheered. I was unlikely to ever meet these people again, but finding ourselves miles from home in a rain-soaked Italian campsite had created an instant bond – the type of intense but fleeting friendships that only occur when you're travelling.

The next day, the question loomed large. Where should I go next? Until this point there had been a purpose to my trip. I had wanted to seek fresh creative inspiration, test my resilience and find out whether I could cope with living in Bambi full time. I'd managed pretty well to date, but now I'd got this far I wasn't quite sure what to do with myself or what path to take next.

In the end I decided to revisit an old haunt and pointed Bambi in the general direction of the Cinque Terre on the Italian Riviera – with a stop in Camogli along the way. I'd first heard of Camogli from my late Aunty Kate, the same aunt who'd given me the vintage 'fantasy handwriting' dress that had led to my friendship with Dorothée back in Brussels. Kate had told me about a road trip that she'd made to Camogli with her best friend Frances in the late 1950s, when the two of them were still young, free and single. This enterprising duo, one a charming Irish blonde and the other a fiery English redhead (no mistaking my aunt), took the picturesque fishing town by storm, turning up in their crisp Horrocks cotton frocks pretending to be restaurant reviewers. The wheeze worked a treat, and they managed to bag themselves a few free meals as well as a bevy of besotted admirers. The story had always stuck in my mind and I was curious to experience for myself the place that I'd seen in Kate's faded photographs.

I arrived in Camogli on 16 June, my mother's birthday. The town really was very lovely, all pastel-painted buildings decorated with *trompe l'oeil* effects and a lovely atmospheric fishing harbour to boot. It was quite a schlep from Aosta though, and I felt very tired by the time I parked up and considered my accommodation options. Italy isn't quite as well set up for motorhomes as France is. There are a few basic places where you can pull up and stay cheaply overnight, but they're not in such plentiful supply nor as well appointed. The alternative is to use proper Italian campsites, which tend to be much more expensive.

It was a hot, sticky afternoon and I didn't really want to waste time looking for a suitable place for Bambi, so I decided to treat myself instead to a couple of nights in one of the family-run seafront hotels. No stylish vintage suitcase for me on this occasion, I'm afraid – I simply stuffed a few things from the van into a plastic carrier bag and checked in. I stretched out on the crisp, cool sheets and quickly dozed off to the magical sound of someone playing medieval recorder music in a nearby apartment. After my siesta, I moseyed out, making a bit of an effort to dress up in honour of my aunt. The woman at reception was evidently shocked by the swift transformation from grungy traveller to sophisticated lady and commented on how different I looked. I immediately regretted that I hadn't made more of an effort with my luggage choice.

If you *would* like to travel in style, try this quick upcycled retro suitcase for a spot of old-school glamour!

Make Your Own Stylish Retro Suitcase

Snap up an old suitcase for a song and cover it in printable reproduction travel labels downloaded from the internet. You can use stickers too, but they're more expensive and it's harder to make them look vintage, which is the look you're going for!

The printed labels usually come in A4 sheets. Cut out each one, then crumple them to make them look a bit battered. Stick onto your suitcase using PVA glue. Once dry, tear at the edges and distress sections with a scouring pad to give them an aged appearance. Rub dark soy sauce into the cracks – it works a treat to recreate the vintage look! These suitcases make great indoor storage too. See the photo in the colour plates.

I drifted through the streets in search of some fresh seafood and chose a little table with a view of the promenade. Glass of wine in hand, I relished the last lovely rays of golden light and watched passers-by stroll along the seafront, making the most of *la passeggiata* – the evening walk. This particularly Italian tradition, which takes place all over the country, from the smallest of villages right through to big cities, is always something of a spectacle. It stems from the Italian verb *passeggiare*, meaning 'to take a leisurely walk', with the emphasis on the walk being slow and sociable. It's a real gathering of the community at the end of the day, providing people with the chance to exchange gossip with friends and neighbours, show off new babies, or simply enjoy the slightly cooler air as the sun goes down. People don't just turn up in jeans and a T-shirt, but make an effort to look their best, taking care with their appearance, fully aware that they're being seen, as it were, in public. That evening, everyone looked strangely beautiful, as though they'd come straight from central casting, all tanned skin and luscious, dark hair. A young courting couple strolled happily hand in hand, an elderly lady walked arm in arm with what could have been her middle-aged daughter, chatting animatedly and greeting others as they progressed. It was just day-to-day life for these people, but I was struck by how exotic it all seemed, how different from the UK, where walking is always undertaken with a purpose or seen as an 'activity' – not to be attempted without an anorak and/or walking boots. Watching this relaxed, companionable evening walk was a wonderful way of winding down. Back at my hotel I fell into a deep sleep, lulled by the rhythm of the waves, dreaming about my spirited auburn-haired aunt stirring up trouble on the streets of Camogli.

When I awoke the next morning, I realised straight away that the market was in full swing. I could sense the unmistakable buzz in the air and hear the vendors on the nearby streets shouting out their sales pitch. You've probably gathered by now that I love a market at any time of the day, in any place in the world. But a market in a pretty Italian town just before lunch with my appetite sharpened and an array of good things to eat probably takes top prize. Stalls jostled for space on the cobbles as the locals went about their shopping. I joined the throng, buying fresh provisions for a picnic. Bright-green pesto, beautifully fragrant tomatoes, velvety blushing peaches and the most energetic, thrusting basil plant I'd ever seen. I also purchased special waterproof sandals, essential if I was to encounter pebbly beaches or muddy riverbeds during my future wild swims.

It was midday and already quite hot, but I'd got the shopping bug and couldn't resist peeking at the lovely loose linen clothes for sale underneath a striped yellow awning. I purchased a vivid emerald dress, perfect for the soaring temperatures and easy to pull on over my head in the tight confines of the van. Perfect holiday clothes. It's essential to have simple-to-wear separates when you're travelling in hotter climes. Here's a top to try for yourself. Make it from a pre-loved duvet or bed sheet and you'll be doing some invaluable recycling too. It can be teamed with the Simple Provençal Skirt (p. 156) to create a perfect travel ensemble!

Make the Sew on the Go Signature Top

This is an unstructured top with no darts to worry about. You can even make the back and front in different fabrics and wear it either way round – a day and evening top in one! The neckline is finished with bias binding, which you can either buy or make yourself. This isn't a project for a beginner, as you do need to know how to attach bias binding in order to complete it. There are lots of different ways of doing this and lots of help on the internet if you've not tackled something like this before. The sleeve cap is finished with a little pleat and a button so that it's not square in appearance. It also gives it a nice little style detail.

This top has an easy fit – draw your pattern onto newspaper or a piece of wallpaper and you can use it again and again. You can also make a toile (an initial roughly made top in cheap calico) first to get a more precise fit if you want to. This top is best made using a sewing machine. See the photo in the colour plates.

You'll need

- A measuring tape
- newspaper, ruler and pencil to make your pattern
- scissors
- around 1.5–2 m of fabric, depending on your size (or use an old sheet or duvet cover)
- chalk or fabric-marker pen
- sewing machine
- an iron
- 2 m of bias binding
- two buttons
- needle and thread

How to make

1. Firstly, you'll need to take some measurements for the pattern:

   - Measure round your bust. Add on 12 cm for ease and seams. Divide the total measurement by four. This will give you your pattern width (W).

   - Measure from the base of your neck down your back to where you want your top to finish and add 5 cm. This will give you your pattern length (L).

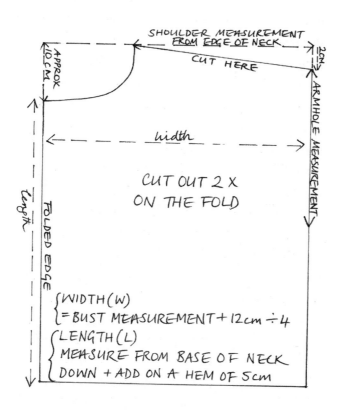

SHOULDER MEASUREMENT FROM EDGE OF NECK

CUT HERE

APPROX 10 CM

2 CM

ARMHOLE MEASUREMENT

width

CUT OUT 2 X
ON THE FOLD

length

FOLDED EDGE

WIDTH (W)
= BUST MEASUREMENT + 12 cm ÷ 4
LENGTH (L)
MEASURE FROM BASE OF NECK
DOWN + ADD ON A HEM OF 5 cm

- Measure from the edge of your neck to down just over the top of your shoulder. This is your shoulder measurement (S).

2. Cut out a piece of newspaper using your L x W measurements. Mark one of the L sides with the words FOLDED EDGE, and the other side UNFOLDED EDGE. Also mark TOP and BOTTOM on the other two shorter sides of the pattern.

3. Take your shoulder (S) measurement and place a mark on the TOP edge of the pattern that number of centimetres in from the UNFOLDED EDGE. Use a ruler to draw a gentle slope from this point down 2cm towards the UNFOLDED edge of the pattern and cut along the line. Then make a smoothly curved neckline from the top of the slope down 10 cm onto the FOLDED edge (see diagram). Cut out.

4. To mark the armhole, measure from the top of your shoulder down under your arm, leaving plenty of room for movement. Mark this on the UNFOLDED edge of the pattern.

5. Right – that's your pattern made!

6. Now fold your fabric right sides together and pin the pattern in place on the fold. Cut out twice so you have a back and a front. Mark the armhole openings clearly on the fabric with chalk or a fabric-marker pen so you remember where they are.

7. Place the back and front pieces of the top together, right sides of the fabric facing, and stitch the shoulder seams with a 1 cm seam allowance. Check that it goes over your head, adjust if necessary, and when you're happy, stay stitch round the neckline close to the edge to stop it stretching. Press.

8. Zigzag (or overlock) each of the remaining sides of the top so that all the edges (including the armhole edges) are neat.

9. Now stitch the sides of the top together using a 1 cm seam allowance (if you want to leave little slits at the bottom, then don't go all the way down to the edge). If you're unsure of the fit, you can always tack in place first before machine stitching. Don't stitch the armholes closed!

10. Turn the top the right way out and press the armhole edges under so they're in line with the rest of the top, machine stitching in place neatly around the edge (you may wish to add bias binding to the armholes instead of turning them under. If so, simply stay-stitch the armholes then add bias binding).

11. Pin the hem and try on. Once you're happy, machine stitch into place, neatening any remaining edges if you've created slits. Finish the neckline with bias binding.

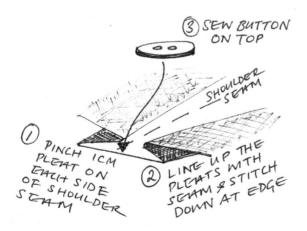

12. Create a small pleat of around 1 cm either side of the top of each armhole (the pleat facing towards the stitch line) and hand sew in place. Stitch a button on top where the two pleats meet. This softens the armhole and prevents it from being too square. (See diagram)

13. You can make this top into a dress too. Just measure round the bottom edge of your top and add on half the amount of fabric again to get the width of fabric you need. Measure down your leg to assess the length (remember to leave on enough for a hem). Gather the fabric up and ease it into the top before hemming the dress to the required length.

I was just stashing my new purchases into Bambi's lockers when a laughing, smiling woman poked her head around the van door. She turned out to be a potter called Elena and had a small studio in Camogli. Her English was a lot better than my Italian, and we quickly fell into an animated conversation about the pleasures and challenges of rejecting the corporate world. She told me how she was struggling to combine her work with motherhood and was startlingly honest about how having a baby and being responsible for the majority of the childcare had meant compromises for her artistic career.

I loved the fact that I was sitting in Bambi, brewing a pot of coffee in the car park talking like this with a total stranger. Bambi often seemed to have this effect on people, morphing into a kind of creative confessional, encouraging visitors to open up and talk about their troubles. On finishing her coffee and her story, Elena ran off to her studio and returned with three tiny clay pots and her phone number in case I got stuck for somewhere to stay. I was so touched. This sort of encounter would never have happened without Bambi.

The Cinque Terre

Think of the Cinque Terre as five exquisite beads on a hand-beaten silver bracelet. I first visited these tiny fishing villages on the Ligurian coast almost twenty-five years ago, and was utterly beguiled by the romantic, soft-hued houses, the tightly winding streets and the stepped olive groves that appeared to cling for dear life to the rugged cliffs as the boats bobbed peacefully at anchor below. I remembered walking the coastal path that linked these pocket-handkerchief-sized communities, feeling my spirits soar and my imagination run riot. I wanted to tap into that inspiration again.

Levanto is known as being base camp for the Cinque Terre. It's not necessarily a destination in itself but it's a convenient place to stay if you want to explore the region. I parked up across from the railway station in a simple camper-van stop with only the most basic of facilities. It was a bit of a gamble, as daytime temperatures were beginning to soar and I knew that Bambi wasn't going to be quite so comfortable in the heat, but I had to be careful about spending too much money.

After securing my pitch, I caught the train to Monterosso, the first of the five villages in the Cinque Terre, with the aim of walking along the coast, just as I had done a quarter of a century before. However, although I was still surrounded by the same stunning vistas, the same azure sea, and the same aromatically perfumed air, I soon discovered that the Cinque Terre's geographical accessibility had made it a victim of its own success. The footpath was now so worn in places that sections of it had been shut due to erosion and there were masses of day trippers vying for space. It was unsustainable and all rather sad – proof, if any were needed, that cheap flights and globalisation come with huge drawbacks. I walked for a while, but soon found the way ahead barred due to a rock fall. I decided to find somewhere to eat instead and got a table at a little open-air restaurant with panoramic views and a tasting menu of various local delicacies. The meal was exquisite, a guilty pleasure. But I found myself feeling slightly forlorn. The sunset was painfully, deliriously beautiful and I couldn't help but think about how I'd hoped to return to this region one day with someone special. Instead, here I was with Bambi, special too of course, but in a rather different way. It saddened me to think that while I seemed able to direct the course of my life in so many other ways, meeting the right person felt completely beyond my control. I'd had several relationships, a couple of them more long-term, but none had ever worked out. Someone had once called me a 'failure' for not having married or had children. Although I'd dismissed this comment (from a man) as stupid, a small trace of what he'd said to me had stuck. What was it about me that had meant I was so single at nearly fifty? My independent attitude? My work? My romantic notions? Possibly all three.

There was only one way to avert this downward emotional spiral, and that was gelato, so I paid my bill and found a little ice-cream parlour down by the shore. I'm not normally an ice-cream fan, but there's something about the Italian version that's completely different and very moreish. Apparently, gelato has much more milk in it than ice cream does and it's usually devoid of eggs too; it's also churned at a much slower rate, resulting in a denser texture. Whatever! The variety of flavours on offer in Italy is simply astonishing! I was overwhelmed when I went to my first proper *gelataria* in Bologna a few years before and was presented with at least twenty different options. Moreover, they all tasted of the actual ingredients, with no trace of artificiality. I developed a passion for the fruit sorbets – so refreshing on a hot day. This time I indulged in three scoops – pineapple and strawberry along with the clean contrast of plain yoghurt ice cream. It was the most intense, creamy and yet refreshing dessert I'd ever tasted. Spirits lifted a little, I pondered an evening dip in the sea, but the prospect of a sticky, salty night in a van with no shower put me off. Back at the camper-van park I was forced to settle for a cold sponge bath behind closed curtains. Ah, the glamour!

Early next morning, fed up of being surrounded by honeymooners (the Cinque Terre is prime couple territory), I decided to go to Florence (I should of course have remembered that this too is a hotspot for young lovers). The man at the ticket office put paid to my belief that Italians are thrilled when you try and speak their language and simply stared at me as I grappled with my dictionary. In the end, he was so rude that I gave up trying to purchase my ticket from him and opted instead for the machine on the platform.

The journey seemed to take for ever, and I finally got to Florence at around midday. The city was heaving and already stupefyingly hot, so after a short while I stopped trying to play the tourist, found myself a fountain-filled piazza, and ordered some lunch. However, instead of being served the snack I'd intended, I'd somehow managed to request two substantial main dishes by mistake – my linguistic skills letting me down for a second time that day. The waitress plonked a huge sizzling steak down in front of me, and my appetite immediately vanished. The parasol offered little protection against the searing sun, which succeeded in sneaking round every corner, no matter how I shifted my seat along. I could feel my skin burning and rivulets of sweat pouring down the inside of my dress. Next to me, in the last sliver of shade, sat a well-groomed English couple. They were sipping champagne and talking loudly about their forthcoming charming Tuscan wedding. I decided that I detested them and that I hated Florence. It may have a reputation as one of the most beautiful cities in the world, but at that particular moment in time, it felt completely unlovely. Every step brought another wave of self-pity. I just couldn't face it. I paid my bill, deciding to cut my losses and catch the train back to Bambi.

The train was no better. The carriages rattled with street hawkers all dodging the guard in an endless game of cat and mouse. Italy seemed shabby and cheap rather than chi-chi and chic – something of a tat magnet. I felt as though all my romantic notions of Italy had been stripped away. I'd been guilty of seeing it through rose-coloured spectacles – a Merchant Ivory version of Italy fixed as a teenager watching Helena Bonham Carter get swept off her feet in a cornfield in *A Room with a View*. I arrived back at the van unable to shift my negative mood, feeling hot and sweaty with the dirt of the city all over me. I just couldn't settle for the night without a proper wash, but the only possible option was the railway station bathroom and I didn't want to go there after dark. There really was no alternative other than to fill a bucket with cold water from the standpipe next to the van and tip its contents straight over my head. It was such a relief that I didn't care what anyone else thought of me, standing there in the middle of the car park, my hair and clothes completely drenched. It almost felt symbolic, as though I was washing away all my unrealistic notions of Italy with a harsh dose of reality.

The odd thing about the travelling life is that you can end up somewhere that's actually quite pleasant without realising it. You arrive at dusk feeling exhausted after the day's drive, locate the nearest campsite or stopover and bed in for the night. The following morning you awake to discover you're marooned in a gravel lay-by, next to a busy road on the outskirts of a seemingly nondescript small town. It might seem like you've messed up, but in fact you've just not had the opportunity to fully explore. This is exactly what happened with Levanto. I'd not given it a proper chance and instead had spent all my time getting the train elsewhere. After my Florentine fiasco, I realised that I'd possibly treated Levanto like the nice boy next door whom I'd completely ignored in favour of his good-looking friend. Levanto was more than a camper-van park next to the railway station. Maybe it was a real gem? It was time to make amends.

Early the next morning, I drove out of the car park onto the road and over the bridge that led to Levanto centre. Scarcely ten minutes away, the smart, tree-lined streets breathed easy in the cool morning air. A sign pointed in the direction of the seafront and soon I was sitting looking out over the ocean, soft sand stretching out to the left and right along the bay. I could just about see the five perched villages of the Cinque Terre emerging slowly through the haze. I absolutely had to go for a swim, so I grabbed my kit and walked down to the beach. The water was gorgeous, even more so after the scorching heat of Florence. There was nobody else in the sea, so I had it all to myself. What a privilege. I swam for a good hour, feeling thoroughly refreshed.

Afterwards, I strolled to a little bar for a drink alongside the locals. Leafing through a well-worn guidebook, I noticed an advert for a proper campsite quite close by. It was a rural haven nestled high up in some olive groves but still within easy striking distance of the town. I finished my coffee and then went to move Bambi. I was just in the nick of time. A rather officious young man was enthusiastically handing out parking tickets, but miraculously he'd not yet slapped one on my windscreen. 'If you leave now, I'll let you off,' he laughed, giving the van an appreciative pat. Bambi had worked her magic once again. People have a hard time being mean when she's around. I threw my damp swimming towel in the back and reversed out, blowing him a grateful kiss.

Camping Acqua Dolce was a little slice of heaven. As it was only mid-June, the holiday season wasn't yet in full swing, so the site was relatively quiet. Up a winding track and behind rusty iron gates, the spacious pitches were banked up on terraces, surrounded by shady palms, bright flowers and gnarled olive trees. The weather was getting hotter and hotter by the day. Today was set to be a scorcher and so, having established base camp, I meandered back down to the beach and splashed out €10 on a luxurious sun lounger and tropical-coloured shade. It was a day for doing nothing. I found a pleasant position on the manicured sand and propped myself up with a copy of Italian *Vogue* (a nod to improving my vocabulary). Around me effortlessly sophisticated people were soaking up the rays and working on the body beautiful, any worry on their tanned faces masked by slick designer sunglasses. Self-conscious, I tried to hide my unshaved legs under my beach towel, but after five minutes I felt so hot I had to throw it off. Why did I find it so hard to relax? I shifted around uncomfortably, feeling terribly English and ungainly in my sensible black one-piece bathing costume.

Looking over the top of my magazine, I noticed a little blonde girl in a frilly white bikini perched on the lounger in front of me, having her hair brushed. She was gazing in rapt admiration at her reflection in a handheld mirror. Every time she returned from a paddle in the sea she was coiffed, dried and dressed in another pristine miniature outfit by her devoted mama. After a while, an elderly couple, obviously family friends, stopped by to chat, gazing adoringly at the little girl. 'How pretty! What a beautiful *principessa* you are!' The child twirled coquettishly, basking in the admiration. *Watch out*! I thought, *You're creating a little monster there*! I laughed at myself. Who was I? Mary Poppins? To Italians, this doting treatment of children is not unusual. They're often dressed like dolls and presented as beautiful accessories. Even though we were at the seaside, I rarely saw children running wild and letting rip. There was a little bit of organised ball-throwing or some beach tennis, but the fun was missing somehow. It was all about *la bella figura* – looking good and fitting in. Unfortunately, all this well-groomed poise made me long for messy hair, flasks of hot tea, windbreaks and sandy sandwiches. I finally admitted defeat, gave up trying to look Italian and threw myself headlong into the sea in a very unruly fashion.

That evening, after a wonderfully reviving shower (what bliss) I dined in solitary splendour at the little picnic table I'd propped up next to Bambi. I cooked myself a large bowl of pasta and smothered it in the fresh pesto I'd bought in Camogli market. Then I washed it all down with a large glass of red wine (red was my only option, given that I had no functioning fridge and warm white is a definite no-no in my books).

I stayed at Camping Acqua Dolce for a few nights, filling my days with swimming and rambling, although my walks along the still-accessible paths of the Cinque Terre had to be confined to late afternoon, when the sting had come out of the sun. When the heat became too much, I sat in the shade and read, my hair swept off my face with a headband made of Suffolk Puffs. They may sound as though they're English cream cakes, but they're actually little fabric circles, stitched around the edges and then gathered at the centre. Create lots of them, and you'll find that the repetitive sewing action is incredibly calming. If you make just two a day for a year, you'll have 730 puffs to play with! My simple-to-make headband features in a photo I took at Camping Aqua Dolce and brings back happy memories of glorious sunshine and the smell of the olive groves. It takes just a handful of Suffolk Puffs to complete this project, and you'll use up your fabric scraps too.

Make a Suffolk Puff Headband and (if you're feeling adventurous) a Suffolk Puff Shrug!

You can fashion anything you like from these little circles once you're confident you can stitch them together securely, even clothes and quilts with a real handcrafted vibe. Try this headband first and then I'll show you how to create my exclusive shrug, which is just the loveliest piece of couture clothing ever! Perfect over a sleeveless summer dress, it really is an heirloom and totally hand sewn as well – not a machine stitch in sight. See the photos in the colour plates.

You'll need

- a compass
- paper
- scraps of fabric (very thick fabrics are not suitable – cotton works well)
- scissors
- pins, needle and thread

How to make a headband

1. Draw a circle on paper with a compass and cut it out. I made a circle 15 cm in diameter.
2. Cut out ten circles of fabric using your paper pattern.
3. Thread your needle with a double thread and tie a knot at the end. Working on the wrong side of the fabric, turn the edge inwards by about 0.25 cm and sew a small running stitch on top of the fold as you go around the edge, turning the fabric over and stitching as you go.
4. When you get back to the start, bring your needle out on the right side of the fabric and pull up the stitches fairly tightly (it'll look like a mini shower cap!) Flatten it down and finish with a secure knot, tucking the ends of the thread inside the puff so they don't show. Now make more puffs in the same way.

5. To sew the puffs together, place two of them back to back (the side with the hole is the front) and overstitch together using a tiny whip stitch. Go up and down for about 1 cm. Knot securely and cut off the thread, hiding the ends inside the puff. Give the puffs a gentle pull to make sure they're secure. Open out and attach the next puff to the first two and so on.

6. As you sew the puffs together, try the headband on for size until you have enough to make it fit securely. Join the ends to make the headband circular.

How to make a shrug

1. The shrug (which will flexibly fit a UK size 10–14) is essentially made from six rows of twelve puffs (made with the same diameter as above).

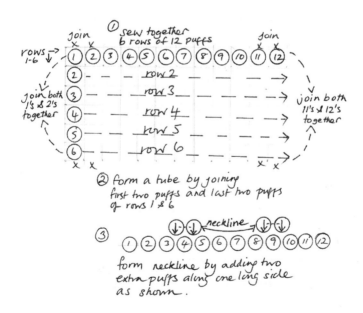

2. First stitch together a row of twelve puffs. Now make another five rows in exactly the same way. Lay the rows out on the floor so you can see how they will all fit together in a grid, one beneath the other. Now join the first row to the second, catching the edges of each of the circles together (just as you did when joining individual puffs). Then join the second row to the third and so on until you have joined all your rows. You'll have an oblong shape made of seventy-two puffs.

3. Fold your oblong in half lengthways and join the first two and last two puffs together (see diagram). You'll see you now have a tube that you can put your arms through at the ends, making a little shrug.

4. Create shaping at the neckline by making two more pairs of puffs. Attach them to the top row of your shrug, as in the diagram. You're done. Good work! Check out the photo in the colour plates for the finished item.

'Ciao Pepe,' came a deep, booming voice from inside a spacious cage positioned next to the reception desk. Proudly perched behind the gilded bars, on a miniature swing, was a splendid blue parrot, obviously making great strides in his mastery of Italian. It turned out that the fabulously feathered Pepe was just a year old and a recent addition to the staff team at the campsite. He was always holding court, surrounded by a group of doting children, who giggled uncontrollably at the sound of his wolf whistles and his star turn, a very life-like imitation of a meowing cat.

I'd already had a surprising start to the day, opening the curtains and quickly grasping for some clothes, as I found the van being photographed by a couple of campers curious to see a wallpapered vehicle with a British number plate parked up next to them.

Now I was sitting in a corner of the on-site café opposite Pepe's cage, a large latte in hand, my map of Europe and my *Wild Swimming* book on the table in front of me. From my vantage point I could comfortably watch the morning routine unfold. Tents were unzipped to reveal their bleary-eyed occupants, while van doors were thrown wide to let in the hint of a breeze. Around me, teams of relaxed-looking cleaners in shorts and T-shirts set off with buckets and mops to refresh the shower blocks. Why was cleaning suddenly looking like an appealing occupation? Snapping on the rubber gloves in drizzly Britain filled me with dread, but here it seemed almost fun.

I gazed at my map. Sometimes I wished that I wasn't responsible for every step of my journey, every single twist and turn. Since leaving the BBC and setting out in Bambi, I'd had complete freedom to go wherever I wanted and yet from time to time the prospect almost paralysed me. Back home I'd sometimes look at my friends in relationships, especially those with children, and envy the fact that they had someone else to orbit around, someone else to help direct them. Was this journey, and especially my experiences in

Italy, challenging my belief that my independence was the most important thing to me? I took a cursory glance at a newspaper and immediately felt the unwelcome presence of the outside world. It was several weeks since I'd read the headlines. The doom and gloom was still out there, but I chose not to consume it. I'd come to the conclusion that whether single or not, life was definitely better when you weren't surrounded by a whole host of problems that you had no hope of solving.

I turned the pages of my *Wild Swimming* book as if I were reading a bible, looking for an answer to a burning question. It fell open at a photo of an idyllic-looking sluice of turquoise water in the Canyon du Verdon in central Provence. My original plan had been to spend much longer in Italy, to drive down as far as the city of Bari on the Adriatic coast and then possibly take the ferry to Croatia, a crossing of some ten hours. However, I was beginning to lose the will to do it. I'd discovered that hitting the road in Bambi in the heat was not as pleasurable an experience as I'd imagined it would be. With no air conditioning, and the engine tucked right beneath my seat, the temperatures in the cab soon became incredibly uncomfortable. It was just like being in a sauna on wheels. The only way to avoid this was to drive at night, something that I wasn't keen to do. I suddenly felt tired, daunted and far from home. What was I doing in this beautiful place alone?

I couldn't rid myself of the nagging feeling that somehow I was filling in time, waiting for my life to start. It was a ridiculous sentiment really. After all, this was my life! I was forty-seven, not twenty-seven, and had already had a successful career as a journalist.

Yet it was almost as though I'd come back to the beginning of a circle. Was I really going to get into Bambi tomorrow and head into the even hotter climes of southern Italy? And what would I do when I got there? I realised I had no idea. I loved Italy, and yet being here was making me feel confused and isolated.

And so the next morning I determined to leave Levanto and go back to France. That turquoise-blue pool in the Canyon du Verdon would be my next destination. I just didn't have the energy to continue further south.

A couple of hours later I was wending my way out of the campsite, Pepe's wolf whistles following me down the road. I passed the temporary parking spot that I'd stayed in only a few nights before when I was unaware that beauty, charm and olive groves lay only moments away. What if I'd never looked? What if I'd driven away thinking that Levanto consisted of a car park next to a station? Sometimes it pays to peer around the next corner and see what lies there, just beyond reach.

7

Heading for the Hills

It was now getting on for the end of June. Temperatures were already higher than average for the time of year and driving the coastal road from Genoa towards France felt like a form of torture. Not only was it incredibly hot, it was also ridiculously windy, the result of the Sirocco blowing across from North Africa. Bambi was pushed hither and thither and I struggled to keep her in a straight line. The engine almost overheated twice and I kept having to stop, as I didn't want further problems with the brakes. Huge trucks bore down on me as I trundled along in my little van, which felt defenceless against the onslaught of the traffic. I passed Genoa, Savona, Finale Ligure – the end of Liguria. Drained from the heat, I stopped at a service station to buy water and peruse my map. Where to aim for? I spotted a few campsites in a place called Imperia, not far from the French border, and decided to spend the night there.

Six hours after leaving lovely Levanto I was nearing the outskirts of not-so beautiful Imperia. It all felt rather unkempt and vaguely threatening. The first campsite I found was not for me, with holidaymakers rammed together like so many sausages under the grill. I carried on and finally pulled into a little place nearer the centre. It was almost seven o'clock in the evening, and I was shaking with the drive, my legs like jelly as I peeled myself from the plastic seat and prised myself from the cab. A quick bite to eat and I hit the sack; all I wanted to do was sleep.

I set off again just after dawn to try and make the most of the slightly cooler conditions. The landscape around me slowly changed as I drove further west. The soft hues of Italian cityscapes merged into high-rise developments, their gleaming panoramas dominating the glittering coastline. I hurtled along the A8 (known as La Provençale) spotting signs for Menton, Cap Martin and Monaco. My make-do-and-mend Bambi felt completely out of place in this millionaires' playground. I eventually passed the huge metropolis that is Nice, but even though it wasn't yet midday, the air in the cab was stifling, with temperatures nearing 40°C. I decided I had to get off the motorway, and took the Route des Pugets at St Laurent-du-Var. To be honest, it wasn't a great choice – I'd just swapped one highway from hell for another. This road followed the course of the Var valley and seemed to go on for ever. The land here was pretty barren, with mountain ranges on either side. My thighs stuck to the seat and I could scarcely breathe, the heat was so oppressive.

It slowly dawned on me that I was very short of petrol. I'd found that in France I was constantly searching for service stations, as they just don't seem to pop up that often. Bambi only does about a hundred miles on a full tank, and so I had to stop fairly regularly to top up. Worried, I asked for directions to the nearest garage from a lorry driver at a lay-by. Luckily it seemed that there was one about twenty minutes away. If I was very careful, I would just about make it. I drove slowly, watching the needle on the fuel gauge drop lower and lower. It was just dipping below zero when I spied not one, but six different petrol stations in the distance, all hugging the same stretch of the carriageway. It was like hitting a fuel mirage in the middle of the desert. Relieved, I pulled in and clambered out to fill up, and was immediately struck by an intense wall of heat. Breaking down in the van here would not have been much fun at all. I stocked up with lots of bread, water and other provisions at the adjoining shop – I had a feeling I was going to need my supplies in the isolated Gorges du Verdon.

Fully laden, I checked my map and keyed 'Roquestéron' into the satnav, a place not too far from the turquoise pool that had become my holy grail. It seemed I'd underestimated the roughness of the terrain though, and soon I was wending my way upwards towards a craggy plateau over poorly maintained roads. Up on the high escarpment of the Estéron valley the roads became narrower, and scattered hamlets clung like limpets to the mountains.

At one point late in the afternoon I took a break to get some further directions. The Alpes-de-Haute-Provence can feel pretty deserted, but even in this far-flung place there was still a local shop selling fresh produce and store-cupboard essentials. I greedily filled a basket with locally grown fruit and vegetables. The helpful woman behind the counter took out a map and showed me a campsite not too far away. Grateful for the tip-off, I got back in the van, Bambi only just clearing the archway that had been blasted into the rock on the way out of the village.

Very tired and weary, I finally found the place I'd been directed to. I'd heard that the campsite was by a river, and so my hopes were high for a swim. The sign pointed down a long, uneven and rather steep track. I crawled along, concerned about Bambi's tyres and the punishing condition of the roads. I really didn't want a puncture now. I eventually pulled up outside what looked like the site office and jumped out to investigate. In a bar opposite was a loud group of bikers all downing beers ferociously and speaking German. They waved me over to the man in charge, who took my details and issued me with a permit for the night. The actual pitch was much further down the track, past a rather spooky, rustic-looking holiday village, which was only sparsely occupied. I have to admit I was a little nervous about being so isolated with a gang of drunken bikers for neighbours, but I had little choice, as I was desperate to stop for the night.

I bumped down the track searching for the river, but there were so many rocks and trees that I couldn't see it. Apart from a couple of caravans, I was the only other vehicle around and there was no mobile-phone signal either. Alarm bells were ringing. I tried to remain positive, came to a halt, and fetched my swimming things. Large limestone crags littered the valley floor, which was covered in brambles and swarming with large flies. I fought my way through and eventually heard the sound of running water. Sure enough, there was a river, but it was very shallow and fast-flowing. It wasn't that easy to reach through the tangle of prickly bushes lining the banks either. My spirits sagged. I wasn't going to be able to swim here and even paddling would be a challenge. I was sodden with sweat and incredibly fed up.

I trudged back to Bambi, insects buzzing around my head. I felt rather vulnerable. I could be trapped down here, murdered and thrown into the river. Nobody would ever know. I made up my mind to head back along the track towards the wooden lodges. It may not have been much more enticing up there, but at least I felt a little less exposed. I spotted a car park nearby, which I'd somehow missed before, and pulled in. There was a fairly elderly gentleman unpacking his shopping from the boot, so I went over to say hello. He had a map of the area in his hand and so I asked him to show me exactly where I was. I was beginning to realise how seriously ill-equipped I was, armed only with a road atlas of Europe – a mistake in this type of terrain, where the satnav doesn't reveal the details of the landscape. I showed him my *Wild Swimming* book and pointed to the place I'd been hoping to reach. It seemed I wasn't quite in the right location, but a couple more hours would get me there. Well, at least that was something; I'd hopefully be able to reach my destination the following day. The man seemed friendly enough and told me he was on holiday. 'You're here on your own?' he asked.

It was a question I didn't usually mind too much, but out here in the sticks I felt rather less confident about proudly proclaiming my solo status. I quickly made up an unlikely story about an artist boyfriend who just happened to have gone off walking for a couple of days while I toured the area in our découpaged van before picking him up. Not terribly convincing, but it was the best I could do off the top of my head. I explained that I'd been hoping to find a place for a swim, but that I'd not been able to get down to the riverbed due to all the prickly thorns, so I was planning to take a shower instead at the campsite. 'Oh,' he said, 'they're not working. You can use mine though, if you like. It's not a problem.' Now, dear reader, I did hesitate. I did stop and think about whether it was a good idea to accept an invitation for a shower in a stranger's house, albeit from a man who must have been in his seventies. But I was horribly hot and sweaty and desperate to cool down a bit. I thanked him, went to get my things from Bambi, and headed over to his hut.

Gerard (let's call him that) seemed intent on giving me the grand tour and pointed out the sitting room, kitchen and bedroom. Thankfully the bathroom seemed to have both frosted glass and a lock on the door, but frankly, by this stage I'd have showered naked underneath a hosepipe in the middle of his garden if I'd had to. I cannot tell you how good it was to feel the water on my skin after the long, arduous drive and impossible heat. I got dried and dressed and surreptitiously headed for the front door. I was just making

my getaway when I spotted a tiny kitten on the pathway, and two
or three others playing nearby. The perfect decoy. I bent down to
stroke them, and Gerard seemed to magically reappear. It was all
a bit Nathalie Lété, like being trapped in one of her rather weird
fairy-tale tableaux.

'Ah! There you are! Do you feel better? You will of course stay
and have an aperitif with me?' Well, what could I say? No thanks,
the shower was great, I'll be off back to my van now?

'Sure,' I said, 'thank you, that's very kind.'

Monsieur generously measured out two very large glasses of
potent pastis and brought them over to the table on the terrace,
where he offered me a seat. 'Do you have ice?' I asked, incredibly
dehydrated after my day on the road. Was he planning on getting
me drunk?

I listened as Gerard told me all about his life. He seemed to have
retired, but I was unclear as to exactly what he'd done beforehand.
After an hour or so of making small talk, I felt that I really had
done my best to be sociable and explained that I had to get back to
Bambi to prepare my evening meal. 'But no! You can't possibly eat
alone. A woman like you? It's far too sad. You must eat here with
me – and you'll join me for breakfast too, of course?'

It never fails to surprise me how ridiculously self-confident some
men are. Was he propositioning me? Or just looking for a bit of
friendly company? I tried to keep it light, thanked him for his kind
offer but explained that I'd spent a very long day behind the wheel
and had lots of food in Bambi that needed eating up. 'Ah, that's not

a problem,' he insisted, 'just bring your dinner over here and you can still eat with me.'

Again, I replied (a little more forcefully this time) that I really needed to have an early night and was very tired. Eventually, looking a little crestfallen, he seemed to accept defeat, but reiterated his desire for me to join him for breakfast. 'You know where to find me if you have any problems overnight, and of course you're welcome to use my bathroom again in the morning,' he said with emphasis, 'if you'd like to.'

I vowed to myself that I would not have any problems – unless they were caused by Gerard himself. I headed back to Bambi, which was parked far too close to his chalet for comfort, but I was stuck. I would just have to stay vigilant in case Gerard came looking for romance once darkness fell. Maybe those bikers would scramble to my aid if I screamed loudly enough.

The night was far from restful. I had to leave the door ajar as it was just too hot to sleep otherwise, but fortunately there was no sign of Gerard. I got up very early, keen to make my escape before I was invited for *le petit déjeuner*. I was curious, though, to see if the showers at the campsite were actually broken. I grabbed my wash bag and walked down to the washrooms. Funnily enough, everything worked perfectly. What a sly old devil Gerard was.

8

Wild Swimming

'In the mountains behind bustling Nice are some of the most spectacular canyons in France … in places, the rivers have eroded deep channels into the rock, creating narrow slot canyons known as "clues". Perhaps the most dramatic in the area is Clue d'Aiglun, off the Route des Crêtes. Here the Estéron River has cut a great silvery cleft in the mountains and emerges in a string of jade.'

Daniel Start, *Wild Swimming France*

The Clue d'Aiglun, which I'd discovered in my *Wild Swimming France* book, had been on my radar for a very long time. I'd often dreamed of diving into the sparkling plunge pools. Now here I was, the opportunity to visit the ultimate wild swim finally within reach.

The Alpes-Maritimes must be one of the most impressive regions of France. A range of craggy mountains crisscrossed by deep gorges and peppered with remote communities, some parts are covered in thick forest while others are parched and desolate. Within minutes of leaving the campsite I found myself high up on narrow tracks carved into the cliff face. There were numerous signs warning about the danger of rockfalls and plenty of evidence to indicate that they often took place. Yet again, I cursed myself for not having a more detailed map, as there was no real way of knowing the altitude of the roads I was travelling on.

It wasn't easy finding the precise location of my swimming spot, but eventually I stumbled upon it more by luck than by judgement. It looked just like its description, a beautiful jade pool carved into the canyon, right next to a bridge about 1.5 km below the village of Aiglun. It was late morning by the time I got there; not ideal, as it was blisteringly hot. I parked Bambi up and stepped out into the scalding heat. I carefully picked my way down the steep, gravelly banks of the river (not the path I was supposed to take) and eventually made it to the bottom, where large, smooth, flat rocks created natural shelves on which to recline after a dip. It was the most amazing natural spa I'd ever seen. I laid out my towel, ready to take the plunge. The water was thrillingly cold and perfectly clear, with chutes and waterfalls that gave an intense natural massage. You could jump into the water upstream and be carried down the rapids just as though you were in a log flume. I wanted to shout out to the world that I'd made it – driven here all the way from London in my wallpapered van!

I swam for a long time, then sat sunning myself on the side, cicadas all around me. Eventually I heard the sound of voices further up the ravine and within minutes an intrepid group bobbed into view, decked from head to toe in their canyoning gear. I'm not quite sure what they made of me nonchalantly dressed in my swimsuit (luckily, I'd thought to put it on), but we exchanged a friendly word or two nonetheless. I soon discovered they'd all come out on a day trip from Castellane, a small town nearby. They clattered past and then made their way up a steep path to the bridge, where a minibus waited to whisk them away.

The sky was clouding over, and so I thought it safest to call it a day too. The water level in these canyons can change very suddenly in a storm and I didn't want to get caught out. After a brief picnic of bread, cheese and tomatoes, I got changed and decided to head to Castellane myself. There was an *aire de camping car* there that would provide a good base.

I'm not quite sure how it happened, but somewhere between Aiglun and Castellane I experienced the most terrifying drive of my life. I found myself on a single track with sheer cliffs on one side and precarious scree on the other, stones tumbling onto the surface of the road ahead of me. I still don't know if I should have been up there at all in a camper van, but if there was a warning sign, I missed it. At one point I encountered a tunnel drilled into the mountain so low that I thought I'd get wedged inside. It was amazing that Bambi passed through it. I started to panic about meeting a car coming in the other direction, because there was no way that I'd have been able to reverse along the tightrope I'd been on. I had flashbacks to my brake problems in Annecy, and realised that if I made one false move, Bambi and I would be over the edge in an instant. I inched along, praying that no other driver would be as insane as me and actually be on the road too. I gripped the steering wheel as if it were a lifebuoy, sweat making it slip in my hands.

That death-defying drive seemed to go on for ever. But by some miracle, I met no other vehicles, and after several kilometres I sensed I was over the worst. The satnav didn't work up there, of course, so I couldn't tell if I was heading even higher up into the mountains or returning to safety. Fortunately, I eventually found myself on a downward trajectory and began to pick up the signal for Castellane again.

I was shaking, my nerves shot to pieces, and I stopped to give myself a chance to recover. I was so relieved to have made it in one piece that I even got out and gave Bambi a hug! There must have been someone looking after me that day because I knew full well that I could easily have come a cropper. The moral of the story is BUY YOURSELF A DETAILED MAP and never venture into remote places without one.

Back down in the valley the landscape became much more verdant, with various swimming spots scattered along the way. But I'd had my fill; all I wanted to do was get to Castellane and settle down for the evening.

I eventually crawled in, pulling up alongside the biggest and most flashy camper van I'd ever seen. But it was my little Bambi that deserved all the honours. She'd brought me safely thus far, in spite of all my recklessness. If Bambi had been a horse, she'd have been given extra rations of hay that night.

The following day I sat down to a delicious breakfast of fresh croissants with apricot jam and a large bowl of milky coffee. I was really living it up! My brush with mortality had jolted me out of the rather gloomy mood that had lingered since Italy, and I felt a new determination to make the most of my trip and appreciate every little detail. I set my sights on the medieval town of Grasse, which is famous for its perfume. I needed to reconnect with the creative purpose of my journey and it seemed like the perfect place to do just that.

9

Perfume

The approach to Grasse doesn't give much away. You'd never think that it's the perfume capital of the world. I'd always imagined the city would be encircled by colourful fields of fragrant flowers, but in fact it's surrounded by the same breeze-block megastores you find everywhere in France. Industrial and built-up, it was hard to believe that the historic *parfumeries* of Molinard, Fragonard and Galimard lay within its walls.

My plan had been to spend the afternoon having a look around, but I soon discovered that I wasn't welcome. Camper vans are not allowed into the centre, and I couldn't see anything resembling a park-and-ride either. At one point I mistakenly headed down a forbidden side street and found myself the victim of a potential road-rage incident with a cacophony of angry car horns blaring at Bambi from every direction.

After what seemed like an age of going round and round in the oppressive heat, I escaped the snarl-up by following directions for a campsite just a few kilometres away. Not too expensive, and with the added bonus of a swimming pool, it was ideally placed for exploring the Côte d'Azur on a budget. While the well-heeled locals of the French Riviera might have preferred their flash cars, I was able to hop on the bus, leaving Bambi safely behind in the shade.

Grasse was originally famous for its leather goods and produced some of the finest handmade gloves in Europe. Indeed, such was the reputation of its craftsmen that the esteemed glove-makers' guild was founded in Grasse in 1614. The smell of tanned leather, however, was not particularly attractive, and high-society customers soon started demanding fragranced gloves to mask the animal odour of the skins. Gloves scented with lavender became all the rage and soon other notes were being added to the mix. Flowers flourished in the Provençal climate, and the perfume industry literally blossomed. As well as lavender, there were abundant quantities of species like jasmine, orange blossom and tuberose available locally too. The fashion for more sophisticated scents proved unstoppable and by the eighteenth century Grasse, with its excellent trade routes, was poised to become the epicentre of the industry.

Galimard is the oldest existing *parfumerie* in Grasse. Founded in 1747 by Jean de Galimard, it supplied the court of Louis XV with olive oil, pomades and perfumes for which he invented some of the first secret formulas. Other perfume houses soon followed in his footsteps. I visited the relatively modern Fragonard, which was established in 1926 in one of the oldest factories in the town. They offered a free tour, which, although rather simplifying the perfume-making process, was a good way of learning about the basics. Just being inside the cool, high-ceilinged, marble-floored building was a treat. Shaded from the blazing heat outside, I soon felt light-headed as I breathed deeply, inhaling the most delicious bouquet of scents.

Some people have a signature soundtrack that reminds them of their journey; I have a signature scent that I bought in the Fragonard boutique. Called Éclat, it contains notes of orange blossom, lemon, saffron, frangipani, gardenia, marshmallow and amber. I could only afford a tiny flacon, but even now, every time I open it and breathe in the floral, slightly tropical and powdery fragrance, I'm back in Grasse on a hot summer's day, drifting through the streets in something of a daze.

If there's a battle for dominance going on in Grasse then, to my mind, Fragonard seems to have won. Some of the most beautiful buildings in the town have been snapped up by the brand. I visited their expertly curated collection of jewellery and clothing from the Arles region. It was fascinating to trace the key textile trends from the eighteenth to the twentieth centuries and see how they were adapted to suit local tastes. Fragonard has focused on incorporating these historic fashion influences into its clothes and interiors collections. Embroidery, needlepoint and quilted elements all bear witness to the traditional techniques of the past, while the colour palette, too, recalls the subtle tones of Provence. I plumped for a generous cotton beach wrap in subdued blues, browns and oranges, a treasured memento of my wild swimming forays.

Although the historic centre of Grasse still retains some of its charm, it's also become a tourist trap with lots of shops selling high-street brands. It seemed such a shame that even the most famous perfume town in the world had succumbed to the lure of mass production. Oh, for the bygone days, when you could no doubt have purchased a single bar of scented triple-milled soap and had it carefully wrapped in crisp tissue paper by a smiling sales assistant. There's nothing to prevent you from making your own soap, of course, and scented candles too. They can all be presented in beautiful packaging and given as gifts. My take on a perfumed present, however, is my vintage-postcard lavender bag, inspired by the perfumes of Provence and the incredible old postcards you find in *brocantes* all over France.

Make a Vintage-Postcard Lavender Bag

Not only do I love the pictures on the front of old postcards, but also the messages and the variety of handwriting styles on the back. Some of the memories of bygone holidays are so poignant. I have one postcard that was sent to a Miss D. Mawson from her friend Beryl, who was holidaying in Morecambe in the UK in 1912 (a very swish seaside resort at the time). She told her pal that the weather had been 'awful' but that she wasn't feeling lonely as a nice young man was staying in the same boarding house as her. I couldn't help but wonder what became of their budding romance. These tantalising glimpses into people's past lives are so compelling that it seems a shame to just put the postcards in a drawer. When I discovered printable A4 cotton sheets that you can put through your home printer, I realised that I could print the postcards and create a lovely personal gift.

Be aware of course, that while only relevant if you're planning to sell commercially, vintage postcards (like any other printed material) are covered by copyright law, so do check the status of your card before you start printing. You can, of course, create a postcard from your own artwork too if you prefer.

You can sew these by hand, but I think they look a bit more professional if you use a sewing machine. See the photo in the colour plates.

You'll need

- an old postcard (or one you've made yourself)
- printable A4 cotton sheets
- pinking shears
- a 10 cm length of narrow ribbon
- dried lavender and a little funnel, if you have one, to fill the bag. If not, use a spoon
- sewing machine, scissors, pins, needle and thread

How to make

1. Print out the back and front of the postcard onto the printable fabric using the manufacturer's instructions. Peel

off the paper backing and cut out, leaving a good margin around the sides.

2. Place the two sides of the fabric postcard together (back to back, with pictures facing outwards) so the edges align. Using the pinking shears, cut across one of the short edges and tuck a loop of ribbon between the layers so the loop sticks out at a right angle. Pin in place.

3. Using the sewing machine, stitch right around the postcard edge and over the ribbon, but leave a little gap somewhere so you can fill the sachet with the lavender (use a funnel if you have one; otherwise just spoon it in).

4. Once full, sew the hole closed carefully so the stitching blends in.

5. Trim round the remaining edges of the lavender bag with the pinking shears to finish.

10

A Cautionary Tale for Digital Nomads

There was quite a contrast between the genteel atmosphere of Grasse and the down-to-earth campsite that had become my temporary home, but I did my best to create a little slice of glamour. I hung my crochet bunting up in the trees and welcomed numerous curious neighbours in for a complimentary hat-styling session and a glass of wine. I even sold copies of my millinery book to two of my guests.

Watching the parade of holidaymakers was a constant source of interest. In a large camper van parked next to mine was a French family with three young children and an enormous shaggy black dog. He was obviously a much-loved pet and spoiled rotten. Every day, in an effort to keep him clean and cool, the dog would be hosed down with a jet of water. He evidently enjoyed it, and the children got a free shower too as he shook the water off his fur coat like a car wash. Then there was the man who was travelling with two elderly dachshunds. They were unable to eat without assistance and so he fed them himself with a spoon, hardly leaving his van as he couldn't bear to be parted from them. There was even a feline holidaymaker on site. An impressive longhaired tortoiseshell cat had arrived with a couple from Milan. She'd be left lounging on the moquette during the day (the window left slightly ajar to ensure enough ventilation) and proudly walked on a lead in the evening. I hope she appreciated her vacation.

Finding a place with a pool was such a bonus, given the ever-increasing temperatures, which were now nudging 45°C. This one also had a restaurant and a bar run by an English eccentric who'd decided to come and live the good life in the South of France. He'd married a local woman, had a couple of kids, and then got divorced. He had no inclination to return to Britain and had recently been promoted from poolside attendant to chef, a role that suited him down to the ground. He was an excellent cook and served up the French classics with panache but could equally do you a great bacon and eggs if you asked nicely. There was something instantly trustworthy about him and it was fun to sit and have an amicable beer together after returning from my various excursions.

Campsites can also attract less salubrious characters and, with a transient population, you never quite know who you're going to meet next. As a woman of a certain age (one seems to become fairly invisible after forty-five), I hadn't bargained on eliciting much attention, although I'd become a little more wary since my encounter with Gerard.

I'd been keeping a regular blog during my travels and I relied on my laptop enormously. My solar charger was rather slow, so since arriving at the campsite I'd got into the habit of plugging my computer into the mains in the communal laundry room instead. I always kept an eye on it, popping in to make sure it didn't disappear. However, the possibility of it being stolen seemed to concern one of the older campers, who offered to charge it up for me himself 'to keep it out of harm's way'. I gladly accepted the generous gesture and was happy to pause for the coffee he offered me when I went to retrieve it.

My new friend filled me in on his life story as he fussed around with the coffee pot and got out a packet of biscuits. He'd apparently netted himself a glamourous girlfriend whilst travelling, but unfortunately, they got to spend very little time together.

'Can I ask you something?' he suddenly blurted out as I poured the milk. 'How do you manage, you know, being on your own such a lot.'

'Manage what?' I enquired, looking at him blankly.

'Well,' he said, without a hint of embarrassment, 'manage. Maybe it's different for women but with my girlfriend far away, I get, you know, frustrated.'

It slowly dawned on me what he might be getting at.

'The trouble is,' he continued unabashed, 'I can't really do it on my own. I feel too guilty. It just doesn't work.'

He then recounted how he'd once met a lovely lady who'd offered to hold his hand as he relieved his frustration. He explained that her company had made it possible for him to... err... perform. There was an awkward silence. He looked down at his mug. I looked at mine. The thought of taking on the role of his 'assistant' filled me with horror. I gave him my most headmistress-y stare.

'I'm sorry,' I said, 'I think you've got the wrong woman here, it's just not for me. It really isn't something I'd be happy with.'

He immediately backtracked, looking rather flustered.

'Oh! I wasn't implying that, of course,' he said. 'I hope you don't mind me talking openly like this.'

'Of course not,' I lied, suggesting that he perhaps Skype his 'girlfriend' and that she might oblige him with a virtual hand-hold. I looked at my watch, made my excuses, picked up my laptop and scarpered. So much for love!

A Little Slice of Cannes Glam

Keeping to a tight budget is always a challenge when you're travelling for an extended period of time, and the French Riviera is notoriously pricey. Although I'd fortunately found budget accommodation, I was still keen to see how the other half lived.

Cannes reeks of glamour. As it was the host city of the eponymous film festival and a magnet for the rich and famous, I couldn't come all this way without checking it out. I started my day with a mini-train tour of the Promenade de la Croisette, which stretches for a good two kilometres along the shores of the Mediterranean. It's a great way to get your bearings in a town that at first seems to consist of nothing but characterless hotels. However, it soon became clear that the hotels were anything but faceless, impressing with their old-school glamour, stunning Art Deco architecture and comprehensive celebrity guest lists. Legendary names like the Martinez, the Miramar and the Carlton slipped by, the twin domes of the latter reputedly modelled on the breasts of Carolina Otero, one of the most famous courtesans of the late nineteenth century. All the hotels had their own extortionate private beaches too, places where the sand was regularly raked and sophisticated cocktails were served to the beautiful people as the sun went down. A stroll past the marinas revealed luxury yachts staffed by professional crews, offering leather-seated luxury and plush-carpeted interiors to their loaded clients.

Then there was the centrepiece, the Palais des Festivals et des Congrès, the focal point for the prize-giving at the Cannes film festival. Here it was fun to spot the handprints of stars like Meryl Streep, Liza Minnelli and Gerard Depardieu set into the concrete.

My favourite part of Cannes, though, had to be the old-town area of Le Suquet, which was once a sleepy fishing village before the money moved in. It had still managed to retain its character, and it was an atmospheric place to wander around. I indulged in my own little bit of luxury, a three-course meal at a quaint and cosy restaurant on the Rue Saint-Antoine offering fresh local seafood cooked in a rich buttery sauce accompanied by half a bottle of

Sancerre. Fabulous. I then hot-footed it back to the bus stop and my campsite, where Bambi was patiently waiting for me. She may not have been the Martinez, but she was by far the most characterful camper van in town.

11

Bambi has a Break

I appreciate that there are much worse places to be holed up than the French Riviera, but even paradise can feel lonely. It had been a few weeks since I'd last seen anyone I knew and I was really missing sharing the evening with like-minded souls. Bambi had essentially been grounded due to the crazy heat – I just couldn't face driving her any further.

Living in Bambi was becoming unbearable too, without any air conditioning. It was now so hot that I couldn't get comfortable inside and the temperature outside was even more ferocious. I would set my little table for breakfast under the shade of a tree, and by the time I'd finished eating, the sun had advanced so much that I was forced to move. I felt unable to do anything: reading was proving too taxing, and sewing was a definite no-no. It was far too hot to hold a needle. I needed an escape.

I Skyped a friend, who told me that she was flying to Padua for a few days' holiday and wondered if I wanted to meet her there. She and two other pals were then going on to Verona. As I had visited neither of these places before, the plan seemed like a good one. From Verona it would only be a short train ride to Venice, a city I've always loved, so I could bolt on a little excursion there too.

Driving there was out of the question. I would be best to leave Bambi behind. I checked with the campsite owners, who were happy to accommodate her. My mind was made up. I stowed her away on their driveway, packing an overnight bag with essentials for the next few days.

It was wonderfully relaxing to go by rail for once. The Med sparkled as I rumbled along, retracing my steps to the Italian border and seeing the coastal towns and cities from a completely different perspective. The desert haze of my previous drive along the motorway had given everything a distorted feel. This time round the skyline seemed a lot more alluring. Of course, it helped that I was sitting in a pleasantly cool train carriage rather than sweltering behind the wheel of my van, scorched air blowing straight onto my face through the open window.

I was due to change trains for Padua at Ventimiglia, where I had to buy the onward portion of my ticket. I wasn't quite sure what I was doing wrong, but I had yet another standoff over my attempts to purchase a fare in Italian. After queuing, I greeted the rather austere-looking ticket clerk with my most charming smile, determined to get it right this time. He glared at me unimpressed and then told me that he couldn't take cards, as the machine was broken... I would have to go and get some money out of the cashpoint. Refusing to be put off, I headed to a hole in the wall a couple of streets away and duly returned, the queue now ten times longer than before and full of effusive, arm-waving Italians all trying to pay. Eventually I reached the front, and repeated my request for a ticket, expectantly proffering a fistful of euros. Without looking up, the clerk turned over the sign on the front of the glass booth. *CHIUSO* it said: closed. 'I'm having my lunch now,' he said, a touch self-satisfied, 'you'll have to wait in line over there.' He waved at another, even longer parallel queue. I tried begging, I tried pleading, but he simply got up and stalked off. I had no choice other than to start all over again. I only caught the train by the skin of my teeth.

Nothing beats seeing familiar faces when you've been travelling on your own for some time and I flung my arms around my three companions as though they'd saved me from drowning. I've known Mel for years. She's a BBC correspondent and Radio 4 presenter. I got to know her when I worked as her producer in Brussels. We've shared many adventures together, travelling all over Europe. Since leaving Brussels, I've felt that rather than me producing her, she's actually producing me, helping me face all sorts of dilemmas over the years. She's proved herself to be a very faithful friend, as well as someone I can have great fun with. Travelling with Mel this time were two of her old university friends, Jill and Julie. I'd met these two high-fliers in the media many times and was delighted to have a ready-made party to join. The girls were eager to hear how Bambi had been getting on, and over a couple of bottles of wine I regaled them with some of the more memorable stories from my trip to date. Bambi's daring exploits up on the treacherous tracks of the Gorges du Verdon were met with looks of horror, as were my narrow escapes from elderly French Lotharios. I relished having an audience after being without one for so long, and I basked in their good-humoured telling-off.

Padua is a stunning university city, home to the thirteenth-century Basilica of St Anthony as well as the famous Scrovegni Chapel with its beautiful Giotto frescos. Seeing these magnificent masterpieces in the company of others was a delight, as was sitting down for a delicious meal afterwards. I'd spent much of my adult life holidaying on my own, sometimes by choice and sometimes through circumstance. However, my feelings of loneliness, particularly in the Cinque Terre, had reminded me of just how important my friends were to me. Perhaps it had taken my road trip to really bring that home.

Padua not only brought company, it also reawakened my creative curiosity. We were staying at the fittingly named Art Hotel, a beautifully restored town villa, home to a collection of vivid paintings and sculptures executed by the owners themselves. But it wasn't only the artwork produced by our proprietress that caught my eye – her clothing was equally arresting. She wore a range of remarkable home-made garments, the majority of which were fashioned from vintage linen and lace tablecloths. She had a way of combining different patterns and textures to create a wonderfully eclectic boho look, which was completely individual and really effective.

Make a Vintage Embroidery-Covered Notebook

Charity shops and second-hand markets are a great place to pick up vintage table linen of all types, as it's no longer deemed fashionable – a real shame in my opinion, as it's incredibly pretty and usually of very good quality. Many of the smaller pieces like tray cloths and table mats feature intricate cutwork, lace and embroidery in beautiful colours. Embroidery was a skill that used to be taught in schools – even I remember learning how to do a French knot and lazy-daisy stitch at the age of eight. These days, embroidery is no longer considered an essential element of a young lady's education, but it's going through something of a resurgence, with trendy kits being snapped up by cool twenty-somethings keen to have a go. Making clothes out of these lovely fabrics is a great idea, but not perhaps within everyone's reach. Instead, I've come up with a much simpler project. This pretty notebook would make a lovely gift. See the photo in the colour plates.

You'll need

- a vintage embroidered tray cloth (linen or cotton – nothing too flimsy, or the glue will show through)
- an iron
- a small hardback notebook or sketchbook
- repositionable spray mount
- clear glue (like UHU)
- scissors
- pencil and ruler
- coloured paper/very thin card for the inside covers

How to make

1. Press your cloth so it's nice and flat with no fold lines – choose which bit of the embroidery you'd like to feature on the front cover, then wrap it around your book to gauge the positioning. Trim back your cloth to fit the book, leaving a 1.5 cm border all the way round.

2. Cover the table with paper (don't use newspaper, as it might mark the tray cloth) and spray mount the front cover of the notebook. Let it go tacky, then place the cloth on top, pressing lightly to make sure there are no air bubbles. Next carefully spray mount the spine and the back, let it go tacky again and then continue gently wrapping and pressing the cloth around the book.

3. Snip the cloth carefully either side of the spine of the book (as illustrated in the diagram), then, opening the book out,

tuck the little tab of fabric down inside the spine at either end.

4. Now snip the cloth at the corners, cutting out the shaded areas on the diagram as shown. Now use a little clear glue to stick down the six folds – again let the glue go a little tacky first.

5. Measure and cut your coloured paper or card to fit across the inside covers. Fold in half and stick sparingly around the edges and on the fold itself using clear glue. Allow to dry. Place your finished notebook under a heavy object to press it flat.

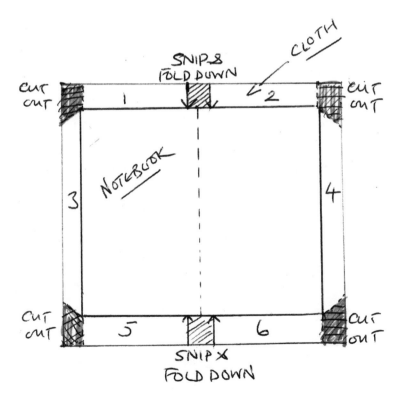

On to Verona, where our goal was to see open-air opera in the magnificent Roman amphitheatre. We managed to get tickets to a production of Verdi's *Aida,* a monumental four-act show about an Ethiopian princess held captive in ancient Egypt. Although the performance was taking place late in the evening, the marble seats were still baking hot from soaking up the day's sun. Fortunately, we were all issued with cushions alongside our tickets, which prevented our thighs from burning and our bottoms from going numb. In addition to the seat pads we were also given tiny candles to light at the start of the opera, just as it was getting dark. The sight of thousands of pinpricks of light glittering around the bowl of the amphitheatre was spectacular, just like floating in a galaxy of stars. It was a remarkable performance, memorable for its sheer scale and ambition as well as the power of the singers' voices. Strolling around the amphitheatre the following day, it was incredible to see vast pieces of scenery and gigantic props strewn over the ground as though an earthquake had taken place. It emphasised the physicality of putting on a production of such epic proportions and the mammoth task the stagehands faced keeping everything in order.

A couple of days later I parted company with my friends, who headed back to London, while I made plans to visit Venice for the day. I'd booked to stay at the Art Hotel in Padua again that night, still only half an hour away by train and a much cheaper option than paying for accommodation in one of the most tourist-filled cities in the world. As expected, Venice was teeming, but for some reason, this didn't bother me the way it had done a few weeks previously in Florence. I stashed my luggage at the station and set out unburdened to immerse myself in the labyrinthine streets and network of canals.

I'll never forget the first time I saw Venice, more than twenty years ago. I'd made the journey by rail and arrived half asleep at Santa Lucia station very early in the morning. Walking through the doors, I felt as though I was stepping into a vibrant film set, with gondolas and vaporetti moored up outside, waiting to carry people across the lagoon to the outlying islands. I had to rub my eyes to check I wasn't dreaming. It seemed so unreal, so utterly beautiful.

During that first trip, I took advice from a guidebook that recommended ignoring expensive sightseeing tours, suggesting instead that visitors should opt for the regular waterbus that slips along the Grand Canal and on to Venice Lido. It remains one of the best ways of getting a sense of this remarkable city. It might be the daily commute for working Venetians, but for holidaymakers it's still shot through with magic and mystery, and there's the added bonus of a sea breeze too.

I disembarked within walking distance of St Mark's Square, the lavish focal point of the city. The air felt increasingly humid and thundery, and sure enough, just as I was standing in the middle of the piazza revelling in the scene, the heavens opened. Within seconds I was soaked through and found myself marooned in the middle of an instant sea. I ran for shelter, ducking under a cathedral archway to wait out the storm. Then just as suddenly as it had started, the rain stopped, and I waded out of my hiding place to bright sunshine and blue skies. Incredibly, I was almost dry within half an hour and able to resume my walking tour as if nothing had happened.

Although Venice is ridiculously overrun with people, somehow you're always able to find a hidden courtyard or an out-of-the-way backwater in which you can enjoy a moment of quiet contemplation. On one particular corner I discovered a lovely shop where they sold handmade marbled paper, a skill I've tried to master many times. I was struck by the complexity of the colours and patterns and bought a packet of offcuts to use in projects back at home. Simply covering a notebook or an empty tin in hand-marbled paper creates a stylish and practical desk accessory.

It was already late by the time I got the train back to Padua. After a quick change of clothes I set off in search of food, passing a shop that I hadn't noticed before. In the dimly lit window were dozens of pairs of beautiful clip-on earrings in the most unusual mix of colours – parrot green with burned orange, crimson red with acid yellow. The boutique was shut, but I made a mental note to come back the following morning to take a closer look. I then found a lively restaurant on a large square where they were serving delicious-looking wood-fired pizzas. The waiters were friendly and solicitous and gave me an open-air table where I could sit and soak up the atmosphere. Afterwards, I strolled back to my hotel, grateful for a comfortable bed and air conditioning.

12

Back to Bambi

I was up in good time the following morning so that I could go and inspect the earrings before leaving Padua. Luckily the shop was open, and turned out to be a real Aladdin's cave, crammed full of all sorts of unusual costume jewellery, most of it second-hand. The earrings had never been worn, all of them dead stock from a Venetian boutique that had closed down after trading for more than half a century. I just couldn't decide on which ones to choose. The earrings dated from the sixties and were made of hundreds of tiny Murano glass beads intricately woven together by hand. In the end I spread my bets and purchased a number of pairs for the bargain price of €10 each. I planned to sell them alongside a range of other vintage goodies at a special pop-up fundraising sale in Bambi once I got back to the UK.

Thrilled with my haul of treasure, I caught a bus to the station, somewhat amused at the sight of the driver, who'd managed to cram his tiny son and daughter into the cab with him for a free ride. Highly illegal, and possibly dangerous, there was nonetheless something about this act of rebellion that I couldn't help but admire. Italians have a real disregard for the rules and refuse to be cowed by bureaucracy. For instance, take the time I travelled from Paris to Rome on the night train. As I propped up the bar with a couple of other passengers, last orders were eventually called, and I thought it meant the end of the party. How wrong I was. That was simply the signal for the bar staff to bring out the home-made wine from under the counter and generously pour a few glasses for remaining guests. Then there was the policeman I saw blatantly lighting up on the platform at Milan railway station, directly beneath the *vietato fumare* (no smoking) sign – completely oblivious to the irony. If I'd witnessed the same thing at home, I'd have been furious, but somehow it seemed strangely acceptable in this part of the world.

It had been fantastic to have company for a few days and to spend a little more time in Italy. Somehow the trip had reignited my love affair with all things Italian and had helped make up for the loneliness that I'd felt in the Cinque Terre. It had also been good to have a break from the driving. Bambi was certainly not proving to be the most relaxing vehicle to take around Europe, but she was still the most characterful, and for that, I was still willing to make a few sacrifices.

On returning to Cannes I received a surprise invitation to go to nearby Antibes for the weekend. My British friend Sarah and her partner were staying in a smart bed and breakfast there, and the owners had given permission for me to park up in their grounds for a couple of nights. It all sounded terribly glamorous. The house and gardens oozed luxury. Built in the late nineteenth century, the white stucco building was tucked away behind electric gates and was surrounded by luscious palms, prolific flowers and fruit trees. Cream canvas loungers bordered a curvaceous swimming pool, and a lazy hammock replete with plump cushions had been slung up in a nearby tree. Bambi and I were directed to a lovely spot underneath a cluster of fragrant pines and in no time at all Sarah and I were catching up over large G & T's clinking with ice.

The B & B owners couldn't have been nicer. They'd arranged to take Sarah and her partner out that evening and very kindly invited me along too. We dined at a swish restaurant and were then driven to Cap d'Antibes, from where we could survey the lights of the bay flickering in the night sky. The following morning we headed to the relaxed Sunday market in the old town and drank coffee at a little outdoor table alongside a group of suntanned local fisherman. The market was overflowing with fresh organic produce and arranged in a way that spoke of both pride and appreciation. I was in my element, gathering a basket-load of good things to share for our picnic lunch following a swim on a secluded beach nearby. As ever, it's the simple things done well that stand the test of time and give us reason to be grateful.

My luxury mini-break was fun, but I'd been in the South of France for almost two weeks (excepting my mad dash back to Italy), so it was high time that I was on the move. I felt rested and ready to take to the road once more. Where to go next, though?

Once again I turned to my *Wild Swimming France* book for inspiration. I'd seen tempting references to a beautiful place called Sillans-la-Cascade, which lay in the mountains behind Cannes. It wasn't a million miles away from the Gorges du Verdon, where I'd had my previous adventure, but fortunately it was much easier to reach.

As it was only 50 km from St Tropez, I hoped to get there fairly quickly, but we were now well into the summer holiday season and the roads were choked with traffic. So I stopped off en route at a little town called Salernes, famed for producing the red hexagonal floor tiles or *tomettes* that are so evocative of Provençal interiors. Once a staple in most homes in the region, you'll now see them splashed on the interiors pages of glossy magazines. Salernes has a very serviceable *aire de camping-car* not far from the centre and so I pulled up there for the evening alongside a couple of other vans. It was a relief to be away from the glare of the coast, tucked up instead in the slightly cooler tree-lined valleys of the interior. I picked up a map from the tourist office and followed the suggested walking trail, admiring handsome carved water troughs, elegant stone fountains and picturesque tile-clad houses. An unusual highlight was the ancient outdoor laundry space, which would once have been alive with the voices of gossiping women scrubbing their sheets and hanging them (and possibly each other) out to dry.

The abundant natural resources surrounding Salernes have been the key to its good fortune and have helped make it a manufacturing success story. Not only is there an ample supply of fresh water and clay-rich soil from which to produce the tiles, but also acres of verdant forest to fuel the kilns. The *tomette* became the principal product of Salernes in around 1850 and found favour not only in the South of France, but also in Italy, Africa and America. The ceramics trade has since expanded to include other products and there are still around fifteen pottery factories employing some 300 people between them.

Having strolled through the town and bought something for my tea, I headed back to Bambi and went to refill my water bottles from the standpipe nearby. As I was doing so, an old man came out of his house, crossed the road and with a friendly smile told me to help myself and take as much water as I wanted. It was a very generous gesture. As I was chatting to him, a pair of curious dogs came to see what I was up to, followed by their owners, a French couple who were parked up next to me in a revamped vintage bus. They'd done all the work themselves. It was very cosy, with a wood-burning stove for the winter and plenty of space for both human and canine passengers alike. The couple didn't know how long they'd live as nomads, but they'd become fed up with paying unaffordable rent and had decided to go off-grid for a while and see how it panned out. I liked their style.

While I was speaking to my temporary neighbours, I was distracted by a man standing under the trees scattering some seed from a paper bag. He gestured to an alternative-looking caravan nearby and told me that the woman living there had rescued a baby bird after finding it on the ground. It had attached itself to her and had never flown far, nesting in a nearby pine. The woman had gone away for a few days and her friend had volunteered to feed the bird instead. It was a touching story. The bird lady was obviously a permanent resident. I thought again of the genial old gentleman across the street who'd so warmly encouraged me to take my fill of water from the communal tap. The fact that he essentially had travellers now living full time across from his house was of no consequence to him. There was no nimbyism in this little corner of south-eastern France. How refreshing and how rare.

The next morning I was up early, determined to get to the famous waterfalls of Sillans-la-Cascade before the heat became too intense. I took special care to top up with petrol as I realised that (yet again) I was heading into slightly unknown territory and I didn't want any more last-minute panics due to lack of fuel. Fortunately there were no hitches and I arrived in good time to buy some breakfast at a café in the attractive little village near the beauty spot. The area was obviously well known for its stunning countryside, as there were lots of hikers already gathering for a day of walking. I asked for directions to the falls at the café and returned to Bambi to fill a rucksack with everything I needed. I locked her up and set off along the path.

After about an hour spent following the course of the river along a steep track into dense woodland, I began to wonder what all the fuss was about. It was certainly a pleasant trail, but I hadn't seen any hint of the cascades. Then I spotted a signpost and eventually heard rather than saw what I was searching for. Guided by the sound of thundering water, I emerged from a slatted walkway onto a wooden platform set high above a huge emerald pool. Plunging into the centre was a spectacular torrent of water surrounded on every side by soaring tufa-lined limestone cliffs, palm trees and luscious trailing plants. The scene was incongruous: it seemed like a snapshot from the Costa Rican rainforest. It was incredibly tempting to scramble down for a swim, but the main path was shut and there were notices up everywhere warning about rock falls in recent months. I decided to be sensible and continued to walk downstream instead to where sections of fast, clear, running water were interspersed with languid pools tinted milky green by the minerals from the limestone.

I had the place pretty much to myself at first but gradually the tranquillity was broken as more and more people arrived to bag themselves a swimming spot. I wouldn't have minded except that some of them were smokers and carelessly tossed their cigarette butts into the water. I couldn't understand why they would come all this way to enjoy such a pristine environment and fill it with litter. Very depressing.

Later that afternoon I drove over to Lac de Sainte-Croix, created in 1974 when the huge Sainte-Croix dam was finished. It's the third largest lake in France, and entirely man-made. Not only does it provide water and electricity to nearby towns and cities, it's also a destination for watersports and sailing enthusiasts. I parked up in Bauduen on the south side, a small village that had once nestled halfway up the mountain. It should have been submerged along with several other places during the construction of the dam. However, unlike its less fortunate neighbours, it had won a reprieve. Since the flooding of the valley floor, it had found a new identity. No longer was it a mountain village but instead a popular lakeside tourist attraction. The water was clear and still, but I have to admit that for me it didn't hold quite the same allure as a river or a natural lake. Nonetheless, I spent a happy couple of hours on the beach watching the antics of a bunch of teenagers who'd brought their incredible diving dog and their friendly pet rat along with them for fun.

After a coffee in a pleasant bar, I consulted my French camper-van guide and located an *aire* not too far away for €7 a night. It even had loos and running water. Quite the four-star hotel! I hopped into Bambi and set out for the other side of the lake, the road climbing higher and higher, eventually finding my destination around a tight hairpin bend. I parked up in one of just two remaining bays, with breathtaking views of the lake below. It was quite something to just sit there with a glass of wine, taking it all in. Later that evening, the last slot in the car park was filled by a rather smart-looking Italian camper van. Out tumbled the family, who were soon setting up a picnic table, dressing a salad and cooking pasta for an al fresco meal. They asked me over to join them, and we all watched the sun set, putting the world to rights in a mixture of French, English and Italian.

The following morning I set off in the direction of Arles. It was a scenic drive, and Bambi pottered happily along through acre after acre of fragrant lavender fields. I passed ancient oak woodlands, many of them fenced off to the public, with 'keep out' signs pasted up everywhere – obviously truffle-hunting gold come autumn. The land here felt rich and fertile. No wonder the produce of Provence was of such excellent quality. And the all-enveloping scent of that lavender! I just had to stop and pick some. It was perfect for filling my postcard lavender bags.

13

Arles

I've always wanted to visit Arles, which was home for a while to the Dutch painter Vincent van Gogh. I'd long been in awe of his paintings and was curious to see for myself what it was about this Spanish-influenced corner of France that had so inspired the artist.

Van Gogh arrived in Arles on 20 February 1888 from Paris, where he'd grown weary of the demands of city life. At first he relished the sun-drenched light of Provence and rented part of a building on Place Lamartine called the Yellow House. He completed several famous works there, including four of his sunflower paintings, as well as *Starry Night Over the Rhône* and *The Bedroom*. Van Gogh planned to turn the Yellow House into a 'studio of the South', a place where other artists could come and work alongside him. In October, Paul Gauguin, whom van Gogh had befriended in Paris, moved in for a while. At first the two got on well, but the tension between them increased and van Gogh became more and more difficult to live with. In December, his mental health issues reached a climax and in a fit of despair he cut off part of his ear and gave it to a prostitute. Gauguin departed, horrified at what had happened, while van Gogh ended up in hospital. Although he was later discharged, he was admitted twice more and eventually, in May 1889, he left Arles for Saint-Rémy, where he was voluntarily committed to an asylum. Van Gogh is believed to have taken his own life in the village of Auvers-sur-Oise in northern France in July 1890, only a year or so after leaving Arles.

There's no doubt that Arles is a charming place, replete with tasteful squares and opulent water features. But I just couldn't stop thinking about van Gogh's state of mind as I roamed the streets. You can go on a walking tour that takes you past several well-known locations, places where he used to set up his easel and paint. I visited the memorable cloistered garden of the hospital where he was incarcerated after severing his ear. The vivid colours of the flower beds exactly matched the ones you can see in the famous painting. I imagined the poor man pacing the grounds battling with his inner demons. The plethora of van Gogh postcards and tourist trinkets felt horribly jarring in this former hospital setting.

Perhaps one of the downsides of being a 'creative type' is that it can make you a bit too sensitive at times. I'd been desperately keen to stop in Arles, but my initial enthusiasm soon became tinged with a pervasive sort of sadness. To be frank, my *arrêt du camping-car* didn't really help much. Essentially a large concrete car park slap bang in the middle of the quayside, it was quite rough, with a dodgy-looking public toilet block the only place to wash. There was a slightly threatening vibe, not helped by having witnessed a vicious fight break out among a group of Roma children. It was almost unbearably hot and sticky and tempers were obviously flaring. The car park seemed to attract a lot of drunk men, and I struggled to get to sleep. Would Bambi's locks hold out if anyone was determined enough to try and break in?

There seemed to be a highly resonant emotional charge in Arles, and it wasn't just me who felt it. I was sitting relaxing by a lovely fountain one afternoon when a very talented guitarist started playing his set. A wistful rendition of 'The NeverEnding Story' suddenly had me in a flood of tears and I found myself weeping inconsolably. Then something quite extraordinary happened. A total stranger came over and planted a single kiss on my head before simply walking off. I was completely taken aback.

It wasn't all pathos. In an effort to jolt myself out of my low spirits, I immersed myself in the crowd at the first-rate Arles flea market, which happened to be taking place during my stay. I just missed out on a stunning faded red straw hat and instead bought a roll of extra-wide pink floral ribbon and a printed Provençal tablecloth skirt in ochre yellow – all colours designed to spread a little holiday happiness. The skirt was so simply made, and yet it served me very well on my travels. A length of pretty material, some elastic and a few lines of stitching is all it takes to sew something similar. Make it in the same fabric as the Sew on the Go Signature

Top (p. 87) and you'll have a matching set that will double up as a shirt-waister dress. You could also stitch a length of patterned ribbon around the bottom of your skirt like I did for an extra slice of Provençal style.

Make a Simple Provençal Skirt

This skirt is perfect if you're new to sewing, as it doesn't require a pattern. The elastic makes it ideal for pulling on and off in the confined space of a camper van *and* it can double up as a changing tent for the beach. It's a wardrobe winner! This is a sewing-machine project.

You'll need
- fabric (around 1.5 m, depending on your size)
- a length of 25 mm-wide elastic
- a measuring tape
- an iron
- sewing machine, scissors, pins, needle, thread
- two safety pins or a bodkin

Fabric calculation
To calculate your waist measurement (W) for the fabric, measure around your waist then add half that measurement

again, plus another 2 cm. For instance, if your waist measures 80 cm all the way around then add 42 cm. So your total waist measurement in this example would be 122 cm. For the length (L), measure from your waist down to the required length, and add on 8 cm. Cut the fabric to this size.

Elastic calculation

To calculate the amount of elastic you need for the waist, take a length of 25 mm-wide elastic. Stretch it around your waist so it feels comfortable and add another 2 cm for overlap. Cut to that length.

How to make

1. With right sides together, sew up the side seam of your skirt using a 1 cm seam allowance. Turn the right way out and press the seam open. The seam will go at the back.

2. To neaten the top edge of the skirt, turn it over to the inside by 1cm and stitch all the way around. Then create a channel for your elastic by turning this edge over again. Make sure the channel is wide enough for the elastic to pass through. Press and pin the channel in place, sewing all the way around just inside the bottom edge. Neaten with a line of stitching just below the top edge too if you can (it helps the waistband lie more smoothly).

3. Unpick the back seam at the waistband just enough to insert your elastic. Safety pin the elastic in place to stop it disappearing and then feed it through the channel using another safety pin or a bodkin. Don't let the elastic get twisted – keep it nice and flat. When you've gone all the

way around, pin the two ends together (overlapping by 2 cm) and hand sew to secure. Remove the pins and stitch the seam closed by hand. Hem the skirt to the desired length.

You can add belt loops too if you wish to hide the elastic!

A second night in Arles passed without incident and the following day I set off again, this time with a mission. I had something of a rendezvous planned. Every year in a small town called Caussade in the Tarn-et-Garonne region of France there's a big hat festival. Caussade is famous for its straw headwear production, and is reputedly the home of the boater, the flat-topped, stiff-brimmed titfer that once graced the heads of both adults and children alike in the late nineteenth and early twentieth centuries. I'd never managed to make it to the festival before, but since studying millinery I'd very much wanted to go, and having driven halfway across France in a van stuffed full of my handmade hats and my books, I was hoping to take part if I could.

The climax of the festival was 19 July, just two days away, so if I wanted to be there in time, I had to get a move on. I decided to follow a route around the coast so that I could avoid crossing the mountains. First, I took the toll road La Languedocienne towards Narbonne, and then headed in the direction of Toulouse, from where Caussade was within reasonable striking distance. I was still finding the driving arduous, and so once I reached Narbonne, I took the A61 and bypassed the city, hoping for a less relentless pace. The landscape changed, stone houses dominated, and red-tiled roofs peppered the scrubby terrain. *Wild Swimming France* promised great things for this region: 'This land of Cathar castles on mountain crags offers great swimming in exquisite rock pools set in verdant gorges. With a rich history, wonderfully hot summers and delicious wines, the Languedoc-Roussillon is a paradise just waiting to be explored.'

One of the places mentioned in the book was Ribaute on the Orbieu River. With its 'fun cascades and longer swims above the weir' it sounded perfect. However, there was nowhere to park Bambi there, so instead I headed for neighbouring Lagrasse which had a cheap and cheerful place for camper vans to stop over.

14

Where the Author Learns Another Lesson or Two

Lagrasse is rated as one of the most beautiful villages in France. It sprang up around the eighth-century Abbey of Sainte-Marie, which is now home to monks from the Benedictine order. It's a picturesque little place with winding medieval streets full of artisans and a surprising number of craft-beer outlets, which are fast becoming more popular in France.

I was lucky enough to arrive just as the weekend Festival des Abracadagrasses was about to start. It's a unique small-scale music event with a wonderfully eclectic programme, one of several cultural happenings that take place in Lagrasse throughout the year. The highlight is a highly regarded piano competition that attracts young musicians from all over Europe.

Arriving in Italy over the Alps

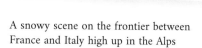

A snowy scene on the frontier between
France and Italy high up in the Alps

Camogli on the
Ligurian coast

The Cinque Terre

Retro Suitcases easily upcycled with printed labels

The Sew on the Go top adds a touch of vintage style to your outfit

Suffolk Puffs are so simple to make and the headband is the perfect travel project

The Suffolk Puff Shrug takes a while longer but it's worth it!

Vintage Postcard Lavender Bags

The Vintage Embroidery-Covered Notebook

Vintage postcards are full of inspiration

High up above the Esteron Valley in France

Lavender fields full of fragrance

A vintage sign painted onto the
wall in Grasse

A water-taxi ride down The Grand
Canal in Venice

The joy of the open road

The domes of the Carlton hotel in
Cannes were reputedly designed to
resemble the breasts of Caroline Otero,
a Belle Epoque beauty

Sew on the Go tea towel designed by Sarah Knight who also created the lovely black and white illustrations for the book.

illustrated by slynknight@hotmail.com

This pet dog sports a hat for Les
Estivales du Chapeau in Caussade

The colours of Provence – perfect for a
simple-to-sew holiday skirt

Popping up at the hat festival
in Caussade was one of the
highlights of the trip

A beautiful old carousel in Arles featuring one
of the bulls that the city is famous for

Cut out simple shapes and hand-stitch them onto fabric to make your own personal scrap banner

Training up the next generation to hunt for bargains

A vintage boater ripe for turning into a quirky clock

Pretty plates can be found in abundance at fleamarkets and are perfect for personalising with transfers

Retro Style Headband

Knot detail from Retro-Style Headband

Takeaway Turbans

Tie your pompoms to lace up boots for a bit of Nomadic Boot Bling!

The North Coast 500 on the
West Coast of Scotland

The St Andrew's Cross or Saltire
is Scotland's national flag

Montrose beach with Scurdie Ness
Lighthouse in the distance

Bambi prepares to take on the Applecross Road

The work of ceramic artist Lotte Glob

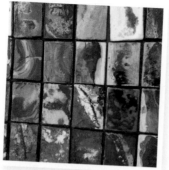

Making friends with Jussi Stader's herd of goats

Montrose Basin at sunset

Durness beach on the far North Westerly coast of Scotland

Make your wall hanging using
things you find beachcombing

Your wall hanging is a lovely
mindful way of creating
textural memories

mantic Travelling Cape

Sew crocheted doilies onto a plain
background for pretty vintage
curtains to filter the light

A pop-up stall in the Old Town during the Edinburgh Festival selling
an amazing stash of 1970s traditional Fair Isle sweaters

Because it was festival time, an expanded campsite had been opened up in an olive grove bordering the village. I was allotted a great spot for just a few euros a night and had a fine time dipping in and out of the nearby river, which forms a wonderful natural lido just under the bridge. I bought a music pass and went to some fantastic concerts, most of which were held in Place de la Halle, a covered fourteenth-century market square that, with its wonderful acoustics and historic atmosphere, made for a dramatic outdoor venue. My favourite event was a gig by the French singer/songwriter Karimouche. One third Jacques Brel, another third Édith Piaf and with a slice of Björk thrown in for good measure, she had fans who'd travelled from all over France to hear her. Being part of that jostling, enraptured crowd, sharing the music was exhilarating, but there was part of me that really wished my friends Mel, Julie and Jill could have been there too. It would have been nice to have had someone to share a drink with afterwards.

I suppose nowhere is ever as idyllic as it seems, is it? Sitting out at a cute little restaurant that first evening, I was just thanking my lucky stars for bringing me to Lagrasse when I spotted an emaciated white dog limping between the tables begging for food. He was obviously in some pain, but nonetheless persevered in his efforts to get a few titbits from the customers. He seemed so hungry that I eventually gave in and offered him some leftovers from my plate. Nobody shooed him away, and later I asked my waitress if she knew anything about him. Apparently he belonged to a local man who lived out in the countryside. The little dog had broken his leg, but the owner had refused to pay to have it sorted out. The waitress shook her head sadly. 'You should take that puppy with you,' she said. 'You could hide him in your van and smuggle him back to Britain.' If only I could have done. I found it sad to think that behind the lovely façade of the village this sort of cruelty was going on seemingly unchecked, just as it does everywhere, of course. A holiday only gives you a very fleeting impression of a community and when you do get a glimpse of 'real life' it can come as something of a shock. I suppose nothing is black or white. Everything is made up of shades of grey, and that goes for people as well as places.

The scales seemed to be dropping from my eyes in all sorts of ways. I'd got to know a couple of French guys in the campsite. I guess they were in their early thirties. They were both great fun and we went swimming together a few times. On the second night they were joined by friends of theirs from Paris, a group of sophisticated, attractive young people who invited me along for a picnic on the riverbank. We all seemed to be getting on well, and they were intrigued to hear more about Bambi. At some point I happened to mention that I was in my late forties, and a sudden hush seemed to descend on the crowd. My new friends stared at me in astonishment. 'We thought you were our sort of age,' said one of my campsite companions. 'Well, I'm flattered you didn't even think to ask!' I laughed.

At first, I was thrilled to have passed for someone more than ten years younger, but as the evening wore on I got the feeling that I was no longer deemed suitable company. I was dropped rather unceremoniously and although we'd been planning to go together, I ended up attending the next gig on my own. As the clock chimed midnight, I left the music behind, feeling a little bit like a middle-aged Cinderella with no glass slipper. At least I had Bambi to act as my carriage. I drove off the next morning in rather a sober mood. I put my foot down, hit the main road that runs from Lagrasse to Toulouse and then headed onwards towards Caussade.

15

Hats and Treasure Hunts

The origins of Caussade's hat industry can be traced back to a thoroughly enterprising local woman called Pétronille Cantecor, who was born in 1770. Legend has it that she married a farmer and spent most of her life cooking, cleaning and bringing up the children. On her rare days outside the home she took on an extra job as a shepherdess and would sit plaiting straw to help pass the time. She started stitching her straw plaits into spirals, making rustic hats for her friends to wear as they worked in the fields under the scorching sun. Soon Pétronille was teaching others her braiding techniques and in 1835 she established a small atelier with her cousin, André Rey. Next to get in on the act was Pétronille's grandson, Jean Cantecor, who opened his own hat factory in nearby Septfonds in 1858. Industrialisation towards the end of the nineteenth century saw the introduction of mechanical sewing machines and steam technology. This meant that hats could be sewn and shaped much more quickly and efficiently. Output quadrupled, and business expanded with the coming of the railway. At its peak, there were some thirty hat factories employing around 2,500 workers in Caussade and Septfonds. It was France's third most productive hat manufacturing region, topped only by Lyon and areas in the northeast of France. Of course, cheap imports affected the hat trade in France just as they did elsewhere in Europe, but the establishment of a factory by Auguste Crambes just after the Second World War meant that Caussade's industry survived better than most. Crambes developed a reputation for smart men's hats and, in fact, the company is still based in Caussade today and exports far and wide.

Crambes is just one of a handful of remaining local hat companies, but the town's reputation as a millinery mecca is intact and continues to attract new talent. Among more recent arrivals is Didier Laforest, who sculpts wooden hat blocks along similar lines to the ones I saw at La Forme in Paris. He moved to Caussade from Chazelles-sur-Lyon (more famous for its felt hats) and now occupies a thirteenth-century building in the old quarter.

Caussade is extremely proud of its unique heritage and refuses to let it die. It's this spirit that has led to the annual international hat festival, which has been taking place now for more than twenty-five years. Every year milliners from all over the world descend to talk shop, exchange ideas, and learn from one another. The highlight of the four-day jamboree is a design competition that attracts entries from as far afield as Japan and has been judged in the past by the likes of Philip Treacy.

I had emailed the festival organisers before setting off from the UK explaining that I would be passing through Caussade in my Mobile Makery around the time of the event and very much wanted to take part in the festivities if I could. Disappointingly, I hadn't heard back, but I was determined to chance it and see if I could gatecrash somehow. The final day of the festival was looming, so it was now or never.

I had broken my journey to Caussade with an overnight stop and I now I found myself just two hours away. I didn't quite know how I'd wheedle my way into the action once I arrived, but I did have my secret weapon with me – Bambi. I pulled into a lay-by on the outskirts of the town so I could pretty myself up. A girl doesn't cross France to attend a hat festival in any old thing! I'd thought a lot about what I should wear in order to create the right impression. I coiled my hair up into my signature 'victory roll' (a vintage hairstyle dating from the Second World War), I put on a lightweight blouse (it was shockingly hot again) and my Mary Jane skirt. I was especially proud of this skirt. I'd designed and made it after doing a screen-printing course in London. Inspired by my Aunt Kate's fantasy handwriting dress, it had my name running in a band around the edge. I completed the look by pinning one of my own 1940s-style creations on top of my head.

Make Your Own Retro-Style Headband

While a straw hat offers perfect protection from the sun, I'm not always in the mood for a big hat. So let me share with you my retro headband pattern. I love it because it's got the feel of a turban, but you don't have to tie it, so it's very simple to wear and exudes a sophisticated forties/fifties vibe. It's also easy to make. This headband looks particularly good teamed with big clip-on earrings, like the ones I found in Padua. You could sew this by hand if you didn't want to use a sewing machine. See photos in the colour plate section.

You'll need

- a narrow plain plastic or metal headband
- some fabric
- a piece of newspaper and a pen to draw a pattern
- measuring tape
- an iron
- sewing machine (optional), pins, scissors, needle and thread

How to make

1. Measure your headband and add on 4 cm to the length. The width needs to be 15 cm at the widest point. Draw a simple lozenge pattern like this onto newspaper and cut out. Pin the pattern onto your fabric (right sides of fabric facing) and cut out two lozenges.
2. For the knot cut out a rectangle 36 cm long and 15 cm wide.

3. Machine stitch the headband fabric together (right sides facing) round the edges (using a narrow seam allowance) leaving a gap of about 6 cm in the middle of one of the sides. Turn the right way out and press. Slip the headband inside and hand sew the gap closed. Gather up the fabric in the centre of the headband and sew to keep it in place.

4. To make the knot, fold the rectangle in half lengthways and sew down one long side (again with a minimal seam allowance) to make a tube. Turn the right way out and press lightly. Tie a loose knot and place over the centre of the headband, folding in the ends underneath. Finish off neatly by hand, trimming off any excess if necessary, and secure in place with a few stitches so the knot doesn't slip around.

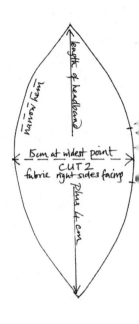

RETRO-STYLE HEADBAND

Outfit sorted (and hopefully now looking the part), I hopped back into the driver's seat and arrived in Caussade around lunchtime, seeing encouraging signs pasted up on the lamp posts advertising 'Les Estivales du Chapeau'. I drew up next to the town square, where I imagined there would be some sort of activity. Sure enough, there were three or four marquees packed with all sorts of millinery paraphernalia, but strangely, no people, apart from one woman who seemed to be looking after everything. I proffered a merry *'bonjour'*, pointed to Bambi and told her that I'd driven all the way from England and was looking for the festival organiser.

If she thought this rather unusual, she certainly didn't show it, and calmly explained to me that everyone was off having lunch in the local sports hall. If I waited a few minutes, she would arrange for me to have a lift out there too. In no time at all, a very affable white-haired gentleman ushered me into his car, and we headed off to the senior-school sports hall, five minutes away.

I shall never forget the incredible surprise I got once I made way inside. It seemed that the whole population of Caussade was having lunch! Among the crowds seated at long communal tables were nearly 200 milliners of all nationalities, chatting away over a delicious-looking buffet and sporting the most eye-catching array of hats. I asked if someone could introduce me to the organiser and was led over to a gregarious-looking older lady on the middle table. I explained my story to her and after a moment's pause, there was a flicker of recognition. Ah yes! She remembered me getting in touch and apologised profusely for not replying. She'd been run off her feet sorting everything out and it had simply slipped her mind. She gave me a warm hug and said she was sure that she could get something sorted out for the afternoon. Perhaps I could park up in the square and do a pop-up there in my van? In the meantime, I was to go and help myself to some lunch.

Their treat. What a welcome. I was over the moon!

Full up from the generous lunch, I was escorted back into town where Bambi and I were guided to a space in the middle of the main square, right next to all the tents. I soon got my pop-up stall ready, arranging my hats and books on a table and making Bambi look her best. She proved an instant hit. The marquees attracted hordes of hatters, eagerly shopping for craft materials and watching masterclasses in a range of different techniques. Before long I was chatting away to both locals and visitors alike, every one of them eager to sit inside and have the 'Bambi experience'. Among my guests was a group of milliners who'd driven all the way over from the Netherlands. They shared my enthusiasm for making a hat pilgrimage to Caussade but, used to rather more high-end transport, were amazed that I'd managed to make it in my tiny, ancient van. Soon we were swapping numbers and I was being invited over to Holland to run workshops in Bambi there. At one point there was immense excitement as a noisy parade passed by. Standing out from all the beautifully themed floats was a plain old farm tractor being proudly driven by a man whose dog sat next to him wearing a mini straw hat with a bright blue bow. Nobody wanted to be left out! Everyone was genuinely welcoming and generous. Not once did anyone complain about me turning up at the last moment and taking a prime slot free of charge at the centre of the festivities.

As the afternoon drew to a close I realised I had sold nearly all my books. I just couldn't believe what a successful day it had been. Eager to try and contribute in some small way, I stayed behind to help dismantle the tents, and by the time I'd finished, I was desperate to cool off. I mentioned to one of the ladies I'd been working with just how unbearable I was finding the heat, and before I knew it, I was being whisked away for a dip in her family pool. Another woman, hearing that I hadn't got anywhere to stay that night, kindly offered me her sofa bed and even gave me a personal tour of the local market the following morning, pointing out the best stalls and produce. I was really impressed by the community spirit in this small town. Nothing seemed too much trouble. It was volunteers who prepared the enormous buffet in the sports hall, volunteers who put up and de-rigged all the tents, and volunteers who offered out their own homes for bed and breakfast to overseas guests. It was all done with a genuine smile and an open heart.

If you're ever near Caussade, then do stop by. You can check out the hat shops and then visit one of the best secret stashes of vintage finds that I've ever come across. Association Iddees on Avenue des Tourondes was stuffed to the rafters with treasures garnered from attics all over France. There were stacks of needlepoint pictures leaning up against the wall (perfect for making my tapestry bags), shelves crammed with vintage glass lampshades, furniture galore, floral curtains, and crates of crockery. Needless to say, I couldn't resist buying one or two vintage bargains as a souvenir of my visit. This project for an old straw boater (quite possibly from Caussade itself) really reminds me of my wonderful stay in the town.

Make a Straw-Boater Clock

I once spied a clock made from a bowler hat hanging on the wall of a millinery supplier's office in Luton and stashed the idea away. When I subsequently saw old-fashioned stiff straw boaters at *brocantes* during my travels in France, I realised that they'd work equally well, perhaps even better, and provide a lovely holiday memory too, once back home.

All you need to make this is a clock mechanism (which you'll find on the internet) and a drill or a pair of scissors to pierce the hat. Find the centre by measuring with a ruler, and carefully make a hole in the middle big enough to take the mechanism. Attach it according to the manufacturer's instructions and add a battery. Use a stick-on loop to hang your clock on the wall – *et voilà*! Incidentally, for a different aesthetic, this project works equally well with a big round wooden Brie box. Just ask nicely at the *fromagerie* and they'll probably give you one for free – alternatively, you can eat your way through an entire Brie and that will do the job too!

Feeling on a complete high, I set off for a tiny town not too far away called Saint-Antonin-Noble-Val, one of the last stops on my French tour.

16

Grapefruit Spoons, Ping-Pong and the Road Back Home

Like Lagrasse, Saint-Antonin-Noble-Val has monastic foundations. Historically, it was a watering hole on the pilgrimage route to Santiago de Compostela in Spain and is home to France's oldest civic building. There are numerous narrow stone alleyways to explore, lots of one-of-a-kind artisan shops and an easily accessible *aire de camping-car* on the edge of town next to the river. On arriving, I waded in alongside one or two other weary travellers seeking some respite from the sun, but soon discovered it wasn't really the sort of water that invited a swim. It was fairly shallow, rather muddy, and teeming with large fish. Good news for the environment perhaps, but not so great for those hoping for a refreshing dip. I perched on a rock instead, dangling my feet in the refreshing current, and soon got talking to a very characterful elderly couple who were also parked up in their (rather smart) camper van in the same place as me. Jeannine, one half of the pair, was very eager to practise her English, having had a British friend called Barbara many years ago at school. Jeannine seemed to have gleaned her knowledge of Britain from a phrase book from the 1950s and spoke in wonderfully accented English about her passion for 'cups of tea', 'cucumber sandwiches' and the Queen. The highlight of our conversation was an animated discussion about grapefruit spoons, which she'd come across for the first time while staying with Barbara's family in London many years before. She'd found the triangular shape and the serrated edge a complete revelation and it had cemented England in her mind as a land of good sense and culture. Maybe a nation's cutlery really does say something important about its place in the world. Jeannine, her husband Pierre and I eventually strolled back to the camper-van park, where we shared an aperitif before I went in search of food.

One of the locals pointed me in the direction of a restaurant called La Guingette de la Plage, a twenty-minute walk away, perched just above the weir. It was a lively place, full of people enjoying the evening sun on the terrace. I wandered up to the bar and ordered a glass of wine, noticing a few tents and the odd camper van pulled up nearby. Although it wasn't officially a campsite, customers of La Guingette were welcome to pitch there as long as they asked nicely and took their rubbish away. I considered moving Bambi but, having already had a tipple too many, decided it might not be wise.

Instead I contented myself with ordering a (very tasty) bite to eat before heading back for the night on foot.

The next morning I did relocate following a pointless exchange with a policewoman about my picnic table. Apparently, erecting my table in the *aire* indicated that I was planning to stay put and I was ordered to pack it away immediately. I found it bizarre, as I'd been eating at my foldable table in *aires* all over France without ever being reprimanded before. All the camper-van owners were in uproar. 'It's just because she's a woman,' muttered Pierre, 'she has to make a point.' I didn't feel quite up to arguing the case with Pierre or the policewoman, so I grudgingly reloaded Bambi and then drove up to laid-back La Guingette, where I bagged myself a spot. I spent the morning kayaking on the river, meandering up and down the banks, but to be honest, it was just too hot to do anything much. Defeated, I hauled the canoe out, had a tingling cold shower under the hose, put on a sundress and spread my towel on the grass ready for a welcome siesta. I soon fell fast asleep under the shade of a tree.

A couple of hours later I awoke with a start to an unfamiliar tapping sound. *Ping. Ping. Ping.* I turned over lazily on the rug and reached for my glasses. Several pairs of tanned and very athletic male legs slowly came into focus. I was surrounded by two dozen incredibly fit men in micro shorts playing outdoor table tennis. The French army had arrived, fresh from their manoeuvres up in the nearby mountains. Needless to say, I spent a very entertaining few hours that evening flirting with the country's finest!

It really wasn't until the last leg of the French part of my adventure that I felt able to pause properly and take stock. I'd clocked up hundreds of miles and often felt that I was on a quest, searching for something but not quite knowing what I was looking for. I was often restless, constantly pushing myself on to the next place and then the next, unable to stay still for long. In truth, I'd replaced the deadlines of the newsroom with ones of my own making.

I had finally reached the Dordogne valley and had discovered a tiny campsite hidden just off the road between Carsac-Aillac and the impressive village of La Roque-Gageac. The site was impeccably clean, with a basic shower block, an outdoor kitchen area and generously spaced pitches punctuated by large shady trees sloping right down to the river. Most of the year the place was mothballed, but every summer the owner carefully mowed the grass, gave everything a fresh lick of paint, and set about earning some money. He would meander along in the morning with a little receipt book, issue each van or tent with a pass for a few euros, doff his cap and wish you all the best for your day. I parked Bambi up just next to the riverbank – so close I could hear the sluicing of water as I slept inside. Here the river was wide, bottle green, deep and quite fast flowing. Low-lying rock plinths on the banks made marble-smooth benches for basking in the sun and I loved diving into the cool depths further upstream and being towed along naturally by the current. When I emerged, my skin felt incredibly soft – it was the best river swim I'd had on my trip. There were no wasps, no mosquitoes, and the weather was perfectly warm without being scorching hot. I felt a huge sense of relief at not having to wage war with the elements.

I stayed in this place for three nights, doing very little apart from swimming, watching the play of light on the water, listening to birdsong and indulging in tranquil afternoon siestas. The river was so soothing it acted as a kind of therapy. I felt a real sense of gratitude steal over me – an attuned stillness and appreciation of the present moment – I suppose it's what you might call mindfulness. My brain was finally able to switch off and literally drift without worrying about the 'where' or the 'why'. I realised I'd actually achieved a lot since setting off. I thought back to the cynical attitude of some of my neighbours in London, scoffing at my plans to take Bambi overseas, and felt immense pride and satisfaction at having proved them wrong. I had shown that I could live a simpler life in Bambi, make connections with complete strangers and work though the episodes of loneliness that had sometimes dogged me. In spite of the challenges, the journey so far had somehow restored my faith, not necessarily in a god, but in a sense of trust, a feeling that I was being guided in the right direction, no matter how random the choices I seemed to make. Maybe my quest was turning out to be the journey itself, and not the final destination.

And now I had come to this place. In a week's time my ferry would leave France, bound for Dover. For once I didn't have to plan anything or look at a map: I knew what was happening next. Before I made the crossing, I was going to spend a few days with my cousins in Brittany. This branch of the family is half French and half Scottish and to keep the French half of their heritage alive, they spend most summers in Carhaix-Plouguer, where they have a house.

There was something of a party atmosphere when I arrived in the town, due to the start of Les Vieilles Charrues, one of the biggest music festivals in the country. However, to my mind, the colourful flags, banners and reams of bunting that festooned the streets had been hung in honour of Bambi. We'd been on the road for more than three months. Apart from my issue with the brakes, I hadn't broken down once and Bambi had looked after me through some very sticky situations. I know it might sound silly to anthropomorphise a vehicle, but so be it. I wish I'd had my own banner as I drove into town that day to proclaim our triumphs to everyone.

Make a Scrap Banner

Banners have a long history. Traditionally made of cloth, they usually convey their message via a symbol, logo or slogan. Think of medieval knights clad in chain mail carrying their banners aloft as they rode their horses into battle, or their use in political rallies today. Making a banner is a great group activity and a good way of showing children how to sew, but creating a personal banner with your own message or slogan is a lovely mindful thing to do too.

I wanted to design a banner that summed up my feelings as I pondered my journey, sitting peacefully by the river in the Dordogne. The message that came to me was 'travel light'. I sewed my banner using some leftover tulle fabric, as it had the feeling of transparency and weightlessness I wanted, but an old piece of net curtain would have been even better. If you're looking for fabric, perhaps track down an old sheet in a charity shop and supersize your slogan!

You'll need
- a length of bamboo and some string
- a piece of fabric
- scraps of material, buttons, beads, etc., for decoration
- scissors, needle and thread

How to make
1. Cut out a piece of fabric the size you want for your banner (you don't even need to worry about hemming if

you don't want to, as this is meant to be a really fuss-free activity).

2. Next, cut out letters to create a slogan that sums up how you feel. The more higgledy-piggledy the letters, the better! Simple motifs like flowers and leaves are also easy to do and look lovely made from scraps of fabric and felt.

3. Sew everything on using a basic 'in and out' tacking stitch or running stitch in nice bright thread.

4. When you've finished your banner, fold over the top and sew a straight line of stitches to create a channel. Slip a piece of bamboo cane through the channel and attach a piece of string. Hang it in the trees and let the wind spread your message far and wide!

I'd grown very fond of my little van during my journey, and I knew that other people had formed an attachment to her too. My relatives in Carhaix were no exception. They felt proud to have Bambi parked on their driveway, and most days we'd spend some time sitting inside on the tea-towel-clad cushions chatting, eating home-made crêpes and toasting a life of 'adventure'. My cousin's husband's father, who'd spent all of his life working on the French railways, was thrilled to have the chance to tinker with a retro van and gave her a bit of much-appreciated TLC, fixing minor issues here and there. Meanwhile I wasted no time in instructing my younger cousins in the ancient art of thrifting – not difficult when there's a fantastic place full of second-hand goodies right on your doorstep.

My cousins had raved about Ti Récup', telling me it 'had MJ written all over it' – and they weren't wrong. It was even bigger than the place I'd visited in Caussade, a vast warehouse just ripe for the plucking. There's something so satisfying about repurposing old materials or giving a pre-loved piece a new home, and it's better for the planet too, of course. There's already enough stuff in the world – a philosophy shared by Ti Récup', which exists to help reduce environmental waste. Since opening in 2012 it has saved nearly 2,000 tonnes of unwanted household goods from being thrown away.

The place is separated into zones for different areas – kitchens and kitchen equipment, sofas and easy chairs, tables and dining chairs, lighting, electrical goods, cutlery, decorative items, and another room for textiles and clothes. I don't know where the seemingly endless stream of vintage goodies comes from, but France certainly seems to have better-quality 'tat' than Britain does. It's getting harder to find rare things, though. I once picked up a pile of thirty 1940s fashion magazines from a similar place for about €5. Now you'd pay that much for each one. However, I still usually manage to uncover some bargain beauties. This time I found a wooden chest of drawers for €20, each drawer fronted with an insert of intricately woven basketwork. I'd seen an identical one being sold at a street market a few weeks previously for nearly ten times that amount. I also purchased a box of lovely old china plates decorated with various flowers and roses. Each one cost less than a euro. These cast-offs are fantastic used just as they are (I love nothing better than serving dinner on mismatched plates) but if you want to, you can upcycle them too. Here's how.

Make Your Own Personalised Plates

Old crockery is to be had by the bucketload from *brocantes* for just a few pence, especially when you're buying odd pieces that don't belong to a set. Take the prettiest plates and turn them into works of art by applying transfers using inkjet waterslide decal paper (you can find it easily on the internet). Print a message or a picture onto the paper following the manufacturer's instructions and then apply as directed. Attach the plates to the walls using Velcro pads or (for heavy plates) wire hangers.

These plates are for decoration only, as this transfer method isn't permanent – but it doesn't matter. They're a lovely way of personalising your finds and putting them on display so others can appreciate them too.

There was time for just one more wild swim before I made my way back to Britain, and this time it was a sea swim. My final night before catching the ferry from Calais was spent in Granville, a fortified town that has, in more recent years, become a genteel seaside resort. The tidal range here is immense. When the sea's out, there are vast swathes of sand to walk over before you reach the water. Closer to hand is a man-made tidal pool, carved into the rock on one side and concreted on the other. In the quiet of the evening it looked extremely inviting. My only other companion was a woman and her golden Labrador. The woman wasn't swimming – it was her dog who was paddling lengths of the pool as she shouted encouraging remarks from the side. He was a real water baby and must have clocked up a few laps before heaving himself out and shaking himself dry. Once they left, I had the place to myself and was able to swim while the gulls wheeled above my head, my slow, purposeful breaststroke rippling the surface of the water as I watched the sun slowly edge towards the horizon, the evening sky tinged with pale pink and orange plumes.

After getting dressed, I installed myself on a little terrace and ordered something to eat, looking out over the sea as the last traces of light faded into dusk. Tomorrow I'd be crossing that same stretch of water back to the UK.

I'd set off with such a feeling of excitement and anticipation, on a high after leaving a job that hadn't been right for a very long time and buoyed up by receiving my BBC severance cheque. The unexpected redundancy money had relieved the financial pressure considerably during my journey – it had freed me from the prospect of having to keep myself afloat by making and selling things along the way. The pop-ups I'd put on in Lille, Brussels and Caussade had been fun and experimental, enough to earn a contribution towards the petrol money but far from providing anything approaching a wage. Fortunately I'd been pretty frugal, buying only the food I needed (I couldn't do otherwise without a fridge), and staying only the odd night in a hotel when the heat overwhelmed me.

Perhaps that's why I'd pretty much suspended the crafting side of things in Italy. I'd found it too hot to think, let alone make anything. I'd also learned that creativity flowed much more readily when I was feeling supported and appreciated (for example in Belgium and France), whereas some of the time in Italy I'd struggled with being on my own. The country's romantic reputation was all well and good if you were in a couple but could make you very aware of your single status if you weren't. I'd felt lost and disconnected in Florence, one of the most beautiful cities in Europe, and it had taken Mel, Julie and Jill to reaffirm that I was still a valued member of a community. Friendship, I saw, was vital to my well-being – just because I was independent didn't mean I always liked being alone. Florence had also underlined that it's not the grand, impressive places that impress me so much as the small, undiscovered ones. In fact the journey had strengthened my desire for a less sophisticated way of life altogether and I realised that some of my happiest moments had been spent swimming in wild places or just allowing myself time to notice the tiny miracles of the natural world.

And of course, there was Bambi herself. I can't underestimate how important a role she played. My journey would have been completely different without her. Her extraordinary appearance was an expression of my own artistic nature, a way of telling the world who I was without even having to open my mouth. I'd spent years working on the BBC news desk looking for a way to fit in, but there was always a part of me that felt constricted. Bambi had changed that completely.

I suppose it was no surprise that the Calais border guards were suspicious of Bambi when I arrived at the ferry terminal the following afternoon. They separated us from the herd and hauled me in for a grilling, obviously believing me to be some sort of drug smuggler. I admit that life on the road had altered my appearance a little. There was the tan, the bright eyes, the sun-bleached hair and the hippy feathers, but surely most criminals would have chosen to travel a little more incognito? An ageing wallpapered van is hardly the perfect getaway vehicle. I tried to explain myself by showing them my craft books and miming sewing actions, but the gendarmes just stared at me nonplussed. They weren't impressed. They were on the brink of strip-searching Bambi (as well as me) when they opened the back door of the van. Out spilled a torrent of old lampshades, cushions, cross-stitched pictures, hats and furniture. They slammed the door shut as if to halt the tide of debris. They had decided it was all too much. I don't think they could face unpacking everything. I was finally ushered onto the boat, the officials left standing on the quayside looking thoroughly dazed and confused as I waved France goodbye.

17

Back Home?

I might have been back on home turf, but my journey was far from over. It was early August, and with my flat still rented out, I was bound for the north-east of Scotland. I was planning to stay there for several months, not in Bambi this time (living in Bambi during the winter would have been impossible), but at my brother's house in the coastal town of Montrose. I hoped to use it as a base for making several smaller excursions while I worked on a new book and tried to carve out a creative future for myself.

Montrose is definitely not one of those quaint little places that you choose because of its obvious charms. At first glance there's not a lot to write home about. There's a large chemicals factory, a harbour that serves the North Sea oil industry and a rather tired-looking high street that's recently spawned a surprising number of nail salons and beauty parlours. But dig beneath the surface, and with time and effort you'll discover a rich seam of artistic and architectural treasures that make it an oddly compelling place to live.

My mother was born in Montrose and in spite of having left as a young woman, she retained a deep and abiding affection for her home town, taking my brothers and me up there for our annual summer holiday until we were all well into our teens. Although it now has a rather neglected air, the natural harbour was once a thriving port, and for hundreds of years it saw trade ships moor up from all over the world. Subsequently, Montrose became home to many prosperous merchants who brought their wealth with them. During the sixteenth and seventeenth centuries they built themselves elegant and imposing houses, many of which are still standing today, tucked out of the way down unassuming narrow closes leading directly off the high street.

During the 1920s Montrose played a central role in the Scottish arts renaissance led by the renowned poet Hugh MacDiarmid, who started out as editor of the *Montrose Review* newspaper. He was the focal point for a distinguished group of other writers and artists all living and working in the area. The sculptor William Lamb had a studio in Montrose, and my grandfather, who was the local vet and a talented artist himself, spent many happy hours there sketching and painting alongside him. The quality of light along this coastline has long been popular with artists – the painter Joan Eardley lived in Catterline, an atmospheric old fishing village just a few miles north of Montrose. Today this part of the world continues to attract many notable talents, including Kim Canale, Stuart Buchanan, David Cook and James Morrison (who sadly died in 2020). All of them draw huge inspiration from the wild, weather-beaten landscape with its wide skies and pounding seas.

For a town where the sea once dominated, it's strange that you can't actually glimpse it from the streets. You have to walk a mile or so over the golf links (Montrose boasts the fifth-oldest golf course in Scotland) and the dunes (many of which have sadly been eroded due to dredging) to reach the beach. But when you do – oh my! It's well worth the wait! When the tide's out, you'll be greeted by a vast stretch of pristine sandy coastline so arresting that the town's current woes vanish in a single buffet of the north-easterly wind. Face the sea and in the near distance you'll get an impressive view of the imposing Scurdie Ness Lighthouse, built in 1870 by David and Thomas Stevenson. It still stands guard over the craggy headland where the South Esk River greets the North Sea, making my heart leap every time I see it.

This place, the town where my mother was born, was to be my temporary home. Having seen first-hand how people loved my little mobile studio, I was keen to find out what further impact she might have in Britain. But there was a more pressing concern too. If I was going to make a living from my creativity, then I would have to get inventive – Bambi needed to earn her keep.

While an undergraduate at the University of St Andrews, I used to take part in various student-theatre productions and then went on to study drama with a view to teaching it. I've always enjoyed performing and for a long time nursed a secret ambition to appear in a play at the Edinburgh Festival Fringe. I thrive in the celebratory atmosphere that lights up Scotland's capital every August, and although I've yet to fulfil the dream of having my own one-woman show, I love watching others tread the boards. The festival started in 1947 with the gratifying aim of 'providing a platform for the flowering of the human spirit' and now visitors come from all over the world to participate both as performers and spectators. For several weeks each year every conceivable venue is requisitioned as an entertainment space (I've even been to a show in a Victorian public toilet) while buskers juggle, joke and stilt-walk their way across the cobbles of the historic Old Town.

Whether you're a performer or the purveyor of street food, if you want to be considered for inclusion in the official festival programme then you need to apply months in advance. As I'd been on the road since April, I'd neglected to do this, but I wasn't going to let a little thing like that stand in my way. I did some research and discovered that there was a new pop-up artisan market taking place in the Old Town during the final two weekends of the festival. I emailed the organisers hoping that, although I was getting in touch rather late in the day, they might nonetheless be on the lookout for unusual traders to attract the crowds.

My plan was to turn Bambi into a mobile shop and sell a stash of vintage sweaters that I'd bought a few months previously from my friend Robin, whose father had once run a knitwear factory in Glasgow. After the business was closed in the mid-seventies, all the unsold stock had been stored in Robin's mum's attic, where it had remained untouched ever since. When the time came to downsize the family home (and knowing that I had an eye for hidden textile treasure), Robin asked me if I'd be interested in buying everything. It was an incredible haul. There were dozens of jumpers and cardigans all made from pure Shetland wool.

The Shetland Isles are just over a hundred miles north of the Scottish mainland and about 190 miles west of Norway. It's thought that sheep were first brought there by Viking settlers, and over the centuries Shetland wool became a prized commodity. In fact, knitting was thought so vital to the local economy that it was taught in schools all over the islands until 2010, when the council voted to remove the £130,000 budget. Various knitwear traditions have emerged from the Shetlands, with Fair Isle designs (which feature intricate patterned bands of two or more colours) perhaps being the most recognisable. During the 1920s the Prince of Wales, who became Edward VIII, boosted the fortunes of the Fair Isle sweater when he wore one on the golf course, and overnight they became the must-have fashion item of the day. My jumpers were definitely influenced by Fair Isle knitting too. The bodies were plain, but they all featured decorative yokes worked in the most glorious range of colours, many including a Norwegian-inspired star design. Apparently, this style became very popular during the 1960s and 1970s, when knitting machines were introduced.

In addition to the knitwear there were also about thirty tartan dresses with finely pleated skirts and soft neckties in muted tones of blue, brown, heather and gold, perfect for channelling that vintage Scottish vibe and cutting a dash at a ceilidh. Every item had been packed in an individual plastic bag, printed with a pleasingly old-fashioned logo, then sandwiched in a brown-paper bundle and tied up with string. The careful storage meant that everything was in pristine condition and, amazingly, there had been no moth damage at all. It was a once-in-a-lifetime discovery and I sensed that both locals and tourists alike would be thrilled with one of these unique garments – a real slice of Scottish fashion history.

Happily, my email to the market organisers was well received, and I was offered a pitch at the Grassmarket. With just a few minor tweaks Bambi was repurposed as a vintage clothes emporium, complete with on-board changing room. Alongside the knitwear and dresses, I also sold some of the beautiful objects I'd found during my travels in France, as well as my handmade hats and signed copies of both of my books. The pop-ups were a huge success and the jumpers and cardigans went down a storm, with customers fascinated to hear the story behind them. I met dozens of people whose mothers or grandmothers had lovingly knitted very similar Fair Isle sweaters for them when they were young, and they were excited to be able to buy something that brought back such fond memories. Of course, it wasn't only the clothes that were a hit. Bambi herself proved a sensation. She received a constant stream of eager visitors and featured in many holiday snaps, everyone intrigued to learn more about her recent adventures abroad.

Make Pom-Pom Bunting and Nomadic Boot Bling!

While I adore my Brocante Bunting (page 66), a different climate and atmosphere demand a different type of decoration. Wool pom-poms suit Scotland, and this garland is fun to make for both adults and children alike. The Boot Bling is a bit of fun and adds a high fashion edge to boring lace-up ankle boots. Read on!

You'll need

- wool in various colours
- a pom-pom maker (or cardboard to make a template)
- small sharp scissors
- a large-eyed blunt needle (a child's plastic needle will be perfect for this)
- a pair of lace-up ankle boots for the boot bling

I don't usually advocate shop-bought instead of home-made, but this is one occasion where I'm going to break my own rules. A plastic pom-pom maker really speeds up the process and doesn't cost much.

If you'd rather make your pom-poms the traditional way, then create a doughnut-style template with a smallish hole in the middle from something like a cereal packet. I like pom-poms that are around 4 cm in diameter. You'll need two of the templates. Put them back to back and then thread your wool in and out through the centre using a thick, blunt needle. Go over and over around the circle, creating even layers, until you can't get the needle through the middle any longer. Cut through the wool all the way along the outside edge of the cardboard and then tie a strand measuring about 15 cm long really tightly around the middle (between the layers of card). Knot it well. Cut off the cardboard and 'hey presto', you'll have a pom-pom!

How to make your bunting

1. Make yourself a good few pom-poms – the more the merrier! I like to mix the colours in each one to get a multi-layered random rainbow effect.
2. Cut off any dangling strands, then thread them one by one onto a long length of wool using your needle.
3. Go right through the middle of the strand of wool, and space them out as you go. They'll stay in place on their own. It's as simple as that!

How to make your Nomadic Boot Bling

To make your boot bling (see the photo in the colour plates) make at least ten pom-poms – five for each boot – but don't cut off the middle yarn quite yet. Instead tie the yarn around a pencil to make a little loop on each one. Make two or three knots so that the loop won't come undone. Snip off any excess. Now take a pair of lace-up boots and unlace them. Loop one little pom-pom over the lace and then do up one hole, then add another pom-pom and do up another hole, and so on. Your boots will suddenly take on the look of a travelling, crafting nomad – which is what you are! They'll add instant winter bohemian chic to any outfit. I promise.

18

Thrifty Travels

From Edinburgh, Bambi and I made our way down south to Lingfield Point near Darlington to take part in the Festival of Thrift, a very special weekend event that's billed as the UK's only national celebration of sustainable living. It's the brainchild of the acclaimed designer Wayne Hemingway, who was the co-founder of the fashion label Red or Dead back in the eighties. I'd been to the festival as a visitor the previous year and had loved it so much that I'd immediately applied to run some ad-hoc workshops there the next time round with Bambi. Even better, I'd been offered a free pitch in exchange for doing a talk and book signing about living stylishly on a shoestring. My moment had arrived!

Lingfield Point was originally built in the late 1940s as the flagship manufacturing base for the Patons and Baldwins wool factory. It was situated in a prime spot on the Stockton to Darlington railway line and quickly became one of the largest knitting-yarn companies in the world. Some sixty years later, following the factory's demise, the site was taken on by a developer called John Orchard, who, rather than raze it to the ground, thought that he'd bring the old buildings back to life in a more imaginative way. He restored the original Art Deco-style details and converted the industrial hub into a creative zone for budding entrepreneurs, exhibitions and even housing. A chance conversation between Hemingway and Orchard led to the concept of a community event at Lingfield Point, and that in turn became the Festival of Thrift.

When I try to describe the Festival of Thrift to friends, I always struggle to paint a comprehensive picture of what goes on there, as it's completely unique. Imagine a two-day party where you'll have fun, learn how to save money, be cannily creative and environmentally savvy, all at the same time. Perhaps it's easier to list some of the things you can do there: make jam with fallen fruit; dance to music that's played by a DJ whose entire repertoire is gleaned from charity-shop LPs; hand print a paper shield with an animal designed by a local artist and then play 'tag' trying to track down those displaying the same creature as you; walk a mile in someone else's shoes (literally); take part in a 'scratch choir'; dine on seasonal home-made food in one of a dozen beautifully curated vintage caravans; build a go-cart from reclaimed materials; learn to cook with smoke; create new musical instruments from old electronic junk; enter an anti-fast-fashion show wearing clothes you've sewn yourself... and that's just the tip of the iceberg!

For my part, I decided to turn Bambi into a mobile millinery booth and offer a 'takeaway turban service', transforming used T-shirts into eminently stylish vintage headgear with the aid of my trusty hand-crank sewing machine.

Make a Five-Minute Takeaway Turban

Fancy having a go? You don't even need a sewing machine to make these beauties. You can do all the stitching by hand and it's a great speedy upcycling project too. See the photo in the colour plate section.

You'll need

- the pattern from this book drawn to scale onto newspaper (see diagram)
- an old T-shirt
- scissors, pins, a sewing machine and/or needle and thread

How to make

1. Turn your T-shirt inside out and place the pattern as directed, so that it lies along the bottom edge of the T-shirt with the side along the folded edge. Pin in place then cut out.
2. Remove pins, then, using a double thread with a knot at the end, gather up the curved edge of the fabric, using a

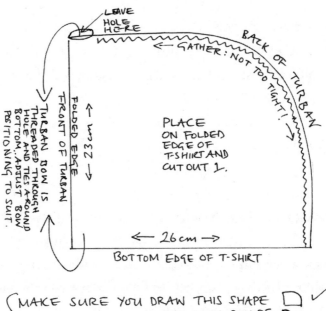

MAKE SURE YOU DRAW THIS SHAPE ⬜ ✓
               NOT THIS SHAPE ⬜ ✗
OR ELSE YOUR HEAD WON'T HAVE ROOM!

backstitch for strength. Don't gather too tightly, as this curve will sit over the back of your head so it mustn't be pulled too small. You can also gather using the sewing machine if you prefer. To do this, set a long stitch length and don't secure the ends of your thread. When you've finished sewing, pull up the threads to gather the fabric, then knot them. Whichever way you choose, make sure you leave a little gap at the top as directed on the pattern.

3. Trim any excess, then turn the turban the right way out. Next take a strip of T-shirt fabric and thread through the hole, tying a bow round the straight part to make the front of the turban. You're done!

The festival attracted some remarkable people, including Jean and Morag, 'the tea ladies with a twist'. I'd seen the Tea Ladies performing at the festival the previous year and was thrilled when someone called us 'style sisters'. Their look is what I'd call 'dressing-up-box chic' – a mash-up of faded floral aprons, sprigged frocks, rollered hair, rose-patterned headscarves and brightly painted pursed lips. They pedal around on a converted tricycle-cum-tea trolley working the crowd and leaving a blurred trail of vivid colour wherever they go. They're not everyone's cup of tea, but I felt very flattered to be compared to them.

Then there were Melanie and Frankie, who immediately caught my eye. The owners of a fancy-dress shop in the north-east of England, they lived and breathed the 1950s, dressing in immaculate period style. But unlike most people who choose to embrace vintage living, they had elevated themselves into a walking, talking, living piece of street theatre by including their dogs in the mix. Their five black poodles, ranging in size from the large Standard through to the ditsy Toy Poodle, were beautifully coiffed and sculpted so that they looked just like the sort of poodles you'd find appliquéd onto the border of a 1950s circle skirt. To see this couple weaving their way through the crowds, clad head to toe in vintage gear and with their five show-stopping dogs on spangled leashes was just wonderful.

The world needs more people like these – creative thinkers who turn their seemingly crazy ideas into something tangible, with flair, enthusiasm and an abundance of imagination.

19

Bambi Goes to the Museum

I was very pleased that I'd tried my Takeaway Turban format at the Festival of Thrift, as it caught the eye of an events programmer from the Imperial War Museum (IWM) in Salford. The northern branch of the IWM was due to host a touring exhibition about the Second World War called 'Fashion on the Ration' and they wanted to book me in for a turban-making workshop themselves. Turbans, usually made from headscarves, were once the fashion choice *du jour* for the girls in the munitions factories, and the look became synonymous with the female war effort. My turban idea fitted in perfectly with the theme of the exhibition, and my focus on recycling chimed with the 'make do and mend' ethos of wartime Britain, which saw people repurpose and repair old clothes to save money and avoid waste.

I could never have imagined that Bambi would one day appear alongside the wartime tanks and planes in one of Britain's most eminent museums, but that's exactly what happened just a few short months later. Stripped of her battery and drained of petrol to ensure that she was no danger to the other priceless exhibits, Bambi was pushed up the steep concrete ramp into the cavernous main exhibition space to take centre stage for a whole weekend.

Yet again I was fascinated by the effect the van had on people. A group of young boys from a Muslim youth club took turns to climb inside and have their photo taken, while a couple of teenage girls expressed their amazement that travelling and living in Bambi might actually be considered a job. For me, one of the best moments came on the Sunday morning when I arrived at the museum early to set up for the workshop. The members of the events team were nowhere to be found. I eventually tracked them down holding their morning meeting in Bambi, sitting side by side on the patchwork benches surrounded by the twinkling fairy lights as if it was the most natural thing in the world. I bet they had a fruitful meeting that day.

20

North Coast 500

Months of writing up in Montrose ticked by. The winter was long, dark and cold and I put on layer upon layer of clothes to keep warm. My brother's house had central heating, but being an old stone building, it took hours to reach a comfortable temperature. With the rental money from my flat in London, the odd freelance writing gig and a smattering of Christmas fairs and craft pop-ups, I managed to keep going financially. Spring saw me heading to Holland to teach a millinery workshop, invited by Elly, one of the lovely women I'd met at the hat festival in Caussade, but it was tough trying to continually come up with ways to pull in anything approaching a regular income. More than anything I wanted to publish a travel-inspired craft book and take people with me on my creative journey, but after trying numerous publishers and receiving rejection after rejection, my spirits were running low.

June 2016 was a milestone. The Brexit bell had tolled and with separation from the EU now on the cards, I felt there had been a severing of sorts. I wanted to run away. While undoubtedly there were many people celebrating the result of the referendum, others were experiencing a sickening sense of disorientation following the vote. I felt a real sense of bereavement and an inability to accept the change that was coming. I'd awake with a start in the middle of the night and after a split second of blissful amnesia, be engulfed by a strange feeling of loss all over again.

I waited for the tide of my mind to turn and the answer eventually came in the form of Scotland's very own Route 66, which takes in some of the country's most spectacular coastal scenery. Now dubbed the North Coast 500 in order to gain tourist traction (much to the dismay of some of the communities that lie along the way), the circular route looks like an old-fashioned dot-to-dot puzzle. The journey starts and ends with Inverness, leading drivers west towards Loch Carron and Applecross, then north via Ullapool to Durness, across to John O'Groats and back down again via the east coast. It's a dramatic and beautiful drive of some 500 miles – just the antidote I needed. A mini road trip in Bambi might just restore my sense of direction.

Before driving to Inverness I decided on the spur of the moment to visit a place called Balmedie, just north of Aberdeen. The small town became famous when a group of local people took on the might of Donald Trump and fought his plans for an eighteen-hole golf course on a specially protected stretch of their coastline.

Sadly Trump won the battle and construction went ahead, but the residents' tireless campaign was captured on film by my brother Anthony, a documentary maker. *You've Been Trumped* won several awards and was dubbed a 'David and Goliath story for the twenty-first century'. I'd met some of the campaigners previously at a screening of the film in Edinburgh back in 2011, but I was interested in visiting Balmedie for myself. Anthony was doing some extra filming there, so it seemed like a good time to tag along.

Anthony had booked into the White Horse Inn and so I phoned ahead to ask if it would be possible for me to stay in the car park overnight in Bambi. Having been given the green light, I set off on a perfect June afternoon, detouring via Balmedie beach before arriving at the inn itself. You reach the wide golden stretch of sand after making your way on foot through a substantial hinterland of dunes. The smell of sun-kissed marram grass was intoxicating, and I lingered for a while inhaling the sweet scent before walking back to the van. It made me angry to think that the Scottish government had been willing to overturn the initial decision by local councillors to reject Trump's plans. So much for protecting this precious habitat.

After parking up at the White Horse, I met my brother and several of the local residents at the bar. I recognised many of them from Anthony's film – Mickey Foote, the former manager of the Clash, his wife Kim, Val, and Susan Munro. Susan arrived looking somewhat flustered, reporting that the pole on which she'd hauled up a Mexican flag (in protest at Trump's latest campaign for his infamous wall on the US border) had been purposely vandalised.

Dark mutterings followed about the ineffectiveness of the police, who'd once controversially arrested my brother while filming, but soon we were on to lighter subjects – including our love of animals. Kim laughed as she described how she was training up a large Newfoundland dog with small treats of cheese in order to keep it to heel. Val, a former teacher, recalled a plump ginger cat that had ruled the roost for many years. She clearly loved him in spite of the fact that he was a bit of a bruiser. The cat would often disappear, and so Val had him fitted with a GPS collar so that she could track him down. On being discovered, he'd happily jump in the back of the car and get a lift back home. It was amazing how this group of people had kept their sense of humour in spite of having their homes circled by bulldozers and their lovely land destroyed.

The following morning brought egg-and-bacon rolls – kindly prepared by the manageress and delivered to Bambi by the chef. A couple of coffees followed and so it was almost midday by the time I bade my farewells and took to the road, striking out towards Inverness via the genteel town of Elgin, home to the Johnstons cashmere factory.

The story of Johnstons is one of determination and commitment. The company was founded in 1797 on the same site that it occupies today. Talk about success in the face of adversity. There have been successive fires and floods over the years, but nothing has stopped the company from growing. Today Johnstons of Elgin is one of the last vertical mills in the UK processing natural fibres from their raw state right through to the finished product. Some of the craftspeople have been employed there for fifty years and the company prides itself on the quality of its work. There's a small museum attached to the main site and it was there that I learned about the history of 'estate tweeds'.

Tweed is a woven wool fabric that incorporates the tones and the textures of the landscape, giving it a real sense of place. The natural palette also means it has a hint of camouflage about it, and as wool is naturally water-resistant, it's also ideal for outdoor wear. By the mid-nineteenth century, as Scotland's clan system diminished, the new lairds adopted tweed as a uniform for the workers who managed the hunting, fishing and shooting rights on their large Highland estates. Individual tweeds with a distinctive weave and colour emerged, enabling employees from neighbouring estates to be distinguished from one another – and so the term 'estate tweeds' was born. I loved the idea of landowners competitively eyeing their neighbours' designs. In fact, it's rumoured that George V (when he was Prince of Wales) rather fell for the jacket of the man next door and asked if he could buy the remaining bolt of fabric. The man refused. He'd had the cloth woven to his exclusive design and the jacket tailored on Savile Row. No way was he going to part with it – not even for the future king!

I toyed with buying a single metre of beautiful (and rather expensive) tweed to turn into a cushion cover, but then, true to my roots as a maker of beautiful things on a meagre budget, I plumped instead for a £15 selection of offcuts to sew into a bargain patchwork version instead. If you fancy having a go at a patchwork cushion cover, then the easiest way is to divide the cover up into equal-sized squares and simply sew a few together. Nine squares is very manageable and will definitely give the impression of patchwork. However, rather than offer you another cushion project here, I'd like to introduce you instead to the joys of weaving.

Visiting Johnstons had really taken me back. My mother used to make my brothers and me small cardboard looms as children and we'd weave using offcuts of wool to form little pieces of multi-coloured cloth. Our attempts would often be turned into miniature rugs for the doll's house or, if they were up to scratch, coasters for mugs. Why couldn't I create a slightly more sophisticated version using the same basic cardboard loom to make little wall hangings?

Make a Mini Woven Wall Hanging

Since returning to Scotland I'd been seduced once again by the rich, peaty tones of the heather-covered moors. I'd also spent hours foraging along the seashore, finding pieces of driftwood, shells and clumps of brightly coloured plastic fishing net muted to bleached tones by the salt water. I loved the idea of blending all these colours and textures somehow. So I made myself a cardboard loom, scoured charity shops for wool, and combined them with my foraged finds. I was really pleased with the results. See the photo in the colour plates.

You'll need

- some strong cardboard
- scissors, a ruler and pen
- sticky tape
- some wool or string
- a comb
- foraged items like driftwood, pieces of dried seaweed, shredded rope, etc.
- a large-eyed needle

How to make

1. First make your loom. Start out with a small one, especially if you're doing this project with children. Cut out a piece of cardboard 16 cm x 8 cm and mark out notches on each short side every centimetre along. This size should give you six notches (it's best to go for an even number of notches, as it helps when you come to tie your wool off at the end). Cut out each notch in a V shape. You'll also need to make a basic little shuttle out of card so that you can wind your wool onto it to weave with. Do this by cutting a strip of card 8 x 2 cm. Snip each of the four corners diagonally and cut a notch in the middle of each short side for the wool. You can wind about 2 m of wool onto your little shuttle.

2. To thread up your loom, start by taping one end of a ball of wool (or string) onto the back, halfway down. Then pass the wool through each of the notches one by one until you've threaded up each of the six warp (vertical) threads. Cut the wool and stick this end onto the back of the loom with sticky tape too.

3. Load up your shuttle with wool and, starting at the top, pass it *over* and *under* the warp threads one after the other. On the second row, do the opposite, passing the wool *under* then *over*. Keep weaving alternate rows. Don't pull too tightly as you weave or you'll distort the shape. Use the comb to push the rows together so that the weaving becomes nice and compact.

4. You can change colours whenever you like. Don't worry about any loose ends – you can sew them in at the end. Experiment by weaving your foraged items into your work as you progress and notice how different textures of wool will give different results.

5. When you've done, cut the strands on the back of your loom through the middle. Tie each pair of warp threads together to stop them all coming undone and use a needle to weave in any loose ends at the back.

6. You can hang the weaving by bunching the top ends together and binding them with a contrasting colour.

The Road to Applecross

My stopover in Elgin was something of a delaying tactic, as I was now bound for Applecross via the North Coast 500, which entailed taking Bambi up on the gruelling Bealach na Ba over Beinn Bhan. This famous route, which means 'pass of the cattle', was used in times gone by to drive herds from Applecross to other parts of the Highlands. It's considered to be one of the toughest roads in Scotland and the internet is full of dire warnings about the challenges of undertaking this legendary pass with its one-in-five gradient and numerous hairpin bends. A large sign at the bottom advises caravans to go the long way round but as I had already successfully navigated Le Col du Petit Saint-Bernard back in France, I was sure that Bealach na Ba would be doable.

Elgin had been sunny and warm, but as Bambi motored west through Inverness and on towards Loch Carron the weather became increasingly stormy. Although the June evenings were long and light, I didn't want to arrive in Applecross, where I'd booked into the campsite, too late. By the time we reached the bottom of the pass, not only was it wet, but it was foggy as well, which made the prospect of the climb a little more challenging. I paused to take a photo, and then started up the famous road.

At first I was able to see glimpses of the stunning scenery to the left of me, but as the going got steeper, the fog became more dense, just as it had done on the drive into Italy over the Alps a few months before. Soon Bambi was crawling along, partly due to the sharp incline but mostly because of the lack of visibility. The track became quite narrow in places, and at one point I had to reverse backwards downhill to allow an oncoming car to pass. I was slightly concerned that we'd go careering over the edge, as I was unable to see a thing. Near the top a couple of roe deer crossed the road right in front of me, barely distinguishable in the mist. I slowed to a snail's pace – it would have been rather ironic for Bambi to run over a deer. Finally we started our descent and the haar lifted enough for me to glimpse Applecross nestled below. It was with some relief that I pulled into the campsite.

I parked Bambi up on the edge of a rather sodden field, where I could just about spy a sliver of the sea through the trees. It was pouring with rain, but I was feeling hungry, so I made for the inn, which was right down by the shore. I arrived dripping wet moments before the kitchen closed, just in the nick of time for a welcome dinner of fish and chips plus a pint from a brewery in Skye. As I ate, I chatted to a young couple, both lawyers, on their honeymoon. The young man had proposed to his wife in Applecross two years previously and they'd come back to celebrate. We discussed our mutual dismay at the Brexit vote, toasted allegiance to Europe and to their long life as a married couple.

After dark I picked my way back to the campsite by torchlight, squelching through the mud to Bambi and, despite the damp, had a surprisingly cosy night's sleep. The next day, after a warming cuppa brewed on the little hob in the van, I continued my journey, with the satnav set to Ullapool. It was still rather dreich and windy, but the coastal road was breathtaking in spite of the poor weather. I paused in the village of Gairloch and then again in Achnasheen to visit Inverewe Garden, which is looked after by the National Trust for Scotland. It's an amazingly lush and verdant spot that boasts a huge variety of species that thrive in their northerly location thanks to the warming effects of the Gulf Stream. It was so tranquil there, and as there was a little break in the weather, I spent some time wandering along the paths through the different levels of the garden. The rain was hammering down again though by the time I reached my next destination, a campsite in Ullapool, so instead of attempting to cook in Bambi, I decided to park up and treat myself to a comforting plate of mince and tatties at one of my favourite haunts, the Ceilidh Place.

The Ceilidh Place

There's something about the Ceilidh Place that makes me feel completely safe. The cosy bar and restaurant boast a huge log-burning stove, there are several well-appointed bedrooms, a cheaper bunkhouse (where I usually stay), an adjoining bookshop, and a wonderfully eclectic residents' lounge full of Scottish paintings. Pick a comfy armchair here and you can while away the hours watching the Caledonian MacBrayne ferry plough back and forth across the water to Stornaway on the Isle of Lewis.

I've spent some happy times at the Ceilidh Place, the most memorable of which was a 'non-Christmas' celebration a few years ago with a group of friends. The rain may have pelted down the entire time then as well, but I was cocooned from the cold with a good book and glass of whisky. My only nod to the outside world was a tiny Christmas tree bedecked with minuscule glass baubles that I surreptitiously placed on my windowsill, having packed it in my suitcase. I'm not sure that this vestige of the traditional

Christmas was really approved of by the owners, but it felt like a small personal symbol of hope in the dark.

With the weather showing no signs of improving, I guiltily abandoned Bambi after one rather miserable night and booked a room, caving in at the thought of a proper mattress and seduced by the memory of all that (non) Christmas cosiness. My contentment at having a warm, comfortable bed should have led to a good night's sleep, but strangely I just couldn't settle. Maybe I'd got used to the regular thrum of the rain on the van roof, but I dozed fitfully, finally getting up when I heard the clatter of the kitchen grinding into action – the full Scottish breakfast that awaited certainly did much to cheer me up.

Before returning to Bambi I wandered around Ullapool's shops and galleries. It might be a small place, but there's a wealth of local creative talent. One boutique stocked a range of recycled goods from much further afield, and at first I was disappointed that Scottish makers weren't represented there. However, I was given such a warm greeting that I instantly forgot my reservations. Who can resist a shopkeeper that engages her customers with a big smile saying, 'Please come in and *really* enjoy looking around'? That's service for you.

A short drive out of Ullapool is the RhueArt Gallery, which is owned by Flick and James Hawkins. It's set in magnificent scenery on the shores of Loch Broom and looks out over the Summer Isles. I was given their address by a mutual friend and decided to pay them a call. I popped in completely unexpectedly, but they made me feel instantly at home. I listened as they recounted their decision to move to this fairly remote part of Scotland in 1978. Our conversation turned upon life choices and the conflicting demands of the creative life. They had certainly made some sound decisions in choosing Ullapool as their base. Not only had James established his own flourishing painting studio, but the couple had also built close relationships with artists from all over the Highlands and Islands. As we talked, a couple of gorgeous husky dogs wandered in and stretched out on the stone floor. They were then joined by the latest addition to the family, an adorable husky puppy who trotted over and nuzzled my hand. The space and freedom seemed immense here, the demands of city living a distant memory.

Durness

It took me a good few hours to drive from Ullapool all the way to Durness on the remote north-westerly tip of Scotland, but I don't think you can do the scenery justice if you make the journey in a hurry. There are arresting views at every turn and it's impossible not to stop and take photographs almost constantly.

The stormy conditions had finally eased, and the sun started to filter through the clouds, casting a magical light on sea and mountain. I arrived at Durness beach in the early evening and parked up on a grassy bank with the sea lapping the shoreline just down below. It was such a peaceful place. A herd of black cattle ambled home along the sand, nibbling on the seaweed as they went.

Waders flocked together in the shallows, calling to one another a
they prepared for the night.

I put on a thick cardigan and went down to the water's edge
picking up dozens of spent limpet shells and occasional curiou
nuggets of hard, garishly coloured plastic, worn completely smooth
by the sea, like crazy neon jewels or a futuristic version of sea glass
I wondered what my friend Jacqueline Lecarme back in Brussel
would have made of these finds. They wouldn't have looked ou
of place in her creations, although they told a worrying story too
about environmental waste.

By the time I'd walked the length of the long beach and returned
to Bambi, I noticed that I'd been joined by one or two more campe
vans, all of us preferring the freedom of this glorious location to
the strictures of the campsite a few miles down the road. I laid
my small table with a pretty cloth and took out a large pape
bag full of Scottish asparagus that I'd bought from a farm sho
near Montrose. I'd been carrying it around with me, determined to
enjoy it in the right place at the right time. I rinsed it and steamed
it in a pan on Bambi's little hob, slathering it with melted butte
before plating up. I accompanied my simple but delicious mea
with a glass of chilled white wine (a cool box works much bette
in Scotland than it does in the heat of southern Europe). Sitting in
Bambi with the door wide open, looking out onto Durness beach
I felt completely at ease, grateful for the gift of such an evening.
watched the sun go down and then made up my bed, falling asleep
easily to the soothing rhythm of the incoming tide. It reminded

me of the calm I'd felt at the campsite in the Dordogne, with the river flowing right past my van. There was something about the proximity to the water that affected me physically, mentally and emotionally – slowing me down, steadying my breath and releasing my anxiety.

What an immense joy it is to wake to a vast stretch of horizon and be able to step straight out of the door into the newly minted morning. I'd like to say I plunged into the sea for a swim too, but I'd be lying. It was one of those days when I was happy to simply look – a vastly underrated activity and vital to the creative process. My eye was drawn to a line etched into the freshly washed sand by the point of an umbrella. An hour or so earlier I'd sat in Bambi, cup of coffee in hand, and watched through the window as a young girl, out for an early walk with her mother, had scored the pristine surface as if forging a path home. This line, like a mark made by a painter on a canvas, led my eye to the far end of the beach, where I could see the herd of cattle from the previous day re-emerging from the dunes. The natural rhythms of time and tide played out all around me. Soon enough that little girl's footsteps would be washed away, the relentless waves would eradicate every trace, and the cycle would begin again. That phrase from my banner came back to me – 'travel light'. We can't control everything, and nothing stays the same. I was striving so hard to find the right direction, but maybe the search for a linear path was not the way forward. Maybe it was all about accepting that life is a collage of many elements, light and shade, ebb and flow.

Just a mile up the road from Durness lies the Balnakeil Craft Village. It's a curious enclave built in the 1950s by the Ministry of Defence as an early-warning station in the event of a nuclear attack. It was decommissioned ten years later, having never been used, and was then acquired by Sutherland District Council with the intention of establishing small-scale industrial units there. This idea never got off the ground, and the place may well have become derelict had it not been for an imaginative council development officer who suggested turning it into a craft destination. Adverts were placed in newspapers all over the UK offering applicants peppercorn rents in exchange for skills and a viable business plan. 'The Far North Project', as it was known, attracted people from all over, and soon the first residents were in situ. It must have been a daunting prospect as well as an exciting one. The bleak concrete barracks had no plumbing or electricity and even after all the hard work needed to create homes and workshops, there was no guarantee that visitors would actually come. But come they did. In the 1980s the tenants were given a chance to buy the buildings themselves and today there are a dozen or so artists and makers still living and working at Balnakeil.

Bambi looked right at home parked up in this alternative setting. Indeed, I'm sure that most visitors thought the van belonged to one of the businesses on site. I made straight for Cocoa Mountain, which is billed as 'probably the most geographically remote chocolate producer in Europe'. A friend, having seen from Facebook that I was heading up to Durness, had suggested that I seek out

Cocoa Mountain, as it served 'the best hot chocolate in the world'. I think it may well have been a contender. Rich and luscious, it came topped with thick whipped chocolate foam and you could even add a couple of fresh truffles alongside your drink if you felt the calorie intake was lacking. It was the most indulgent breakfast I've ever had – perhaps not one I'd want every day, but definitely worth the detour if you happen to be passing!

While many people dream of living in a remote outpost like this, set among stunning scenery, I doubt it's as idyllic as it might seem. Balnakeil is not exactly a cosy spot. It's quite challenging architecturally and geographically, and I imagine you have to be made of fairly sturdy stuff to cope in the winter. Speaking to some of the artists, I got the impression that although they found the place hugely inspiring, it could also prove difficult at times. Until 1986 Balnakeil ran as a co-operative, but nowadays a rota for mowing the grass is the only remaining nod to communal living. I got chatting to painter Ishbel Macdonald, who'd lived and worked at Balnakeil for more than thirty years and had seen many hopefuls come and go. She spent half the year there, choosing to be with her partner in Iceland for the remaining six months. As we spoke, she described the bleak Icelandic winter, which meant about four hours of daylight at most. I suppose that in comparison, Balnakeil must have felt like a pushover.

On my way back to Bambi I noticed that one of the live/work spaces was for sale. A former bookshop, it was the only place in the village to have central heating and boasted three bedrooms.

Wouldn't it have been a fitting conclusion to my adventures if I'd bought the place and lived there happily ever after? For a fleeting second, I was tempted – £95,000 was a price I could afford if I sold my flat in London. Then I wondered how I'd cope in winter when the beach lay shrouded in darkness for nearly twenty-four hours a day and the only contact with my neighbours was the grass-cutting rota. I shivered. It wasn't for me.

Lotte

While chatting to the artists, I asked about finding Lotte Glob's studio. Lotte, a Danish ceramicist, used to live and work at Balnakeil but had since relocated a few miles away to Loch Eriboll, where she'd created an award-winning sculpture croft. I was curious to see her work and decided to check her out.

It was an unforgettable drive from Balnakeil. From high up on the headland I spied beach after bleached sandy beach, daubs of chalky white layered with luminescent aquamarine. Bathed in sun, the panorama wouldn't have looked out of place in a luxury island-hopping holiday brochure, but even on a cloudy day it was still deceptively exotic-looking. Lotte's well-signposted HQ was reached by way of a narrow road, which hugged the loch most of the way. The studio and house complex were striking, their sparse timber structures both blending in with and standing apart from their surroundings. Raised on stilts, the house had the look of an insect hotel, with a stash of neatly stacked logs stored underneath. The natural garden was punctuated by sculptures, with a swathe of paths leading from one focal point to the other, while newly planted trees promised a future woodland.

Back in the studio I decided to buy one of Lotte's tactile three-dimensional tiles, a small work of art packed with earthy colour and translucent glaze – £40 seemed a reasonable price for something so engaging and beautiful. Sadly, I didn't get to meet Lotte herself, but instead spoke to her assistant Josie, who was working there that day. As I chatted, I found myself blurting out my whole story, explaining that I'd been living up in Montrose for several months after travelling in my mobile craft studio. I described how much I longed for a resolution of sorts in my life, but that I never seemed to find it. She followed me back to the van, curious to take a look at Bambi for herself, and I could tell that she was immediately taken with her.

Noticing my haul of beachcombed finds from Durness, she remarked that she'd never seen anything like my plastic jewels washed up before. 'It's a sign,' she said. 'Just when you feel like giving up, the universe throws you something out of the ordinary to show that you have to keep going, that you mustn't jack it all in. Don't water down your vision. Stick to your instincts and don't compromise your creative integrity.' Her words were exactly what I needed to hear. It's often easier talking honestly to complete strangers, knowing that your paths are never likely to cross again. I remembered my chance meeting with Elena, the potter in Camogli who'd hopped on board Bambi and started discussing her life with me so openly; the septuagenarian cyclists in the campsite in Aosta who'd pulled me out of my depression by offering me a convivial glass of wine; and the like-minded couple I'd spent starry evenings with at Lac de Narlay – all of them had given me a little boost at a crucial moment.

Jussi

I had just two more days left to explore the North Coast 500 and so I decided that rather than cram in a whistle-stop tour of the easterly half, I'd linger on the west coast instead and head to the village of Bettyhill. There I hoped to meet a woman called Jussi Stader, who'd moved to the area with her family a few years beforehand to become a goat farmer and cheese maker. I'd been given her number by my friend Kathleen, a life coach from Edinburgh. I think she felt we'd both inspire each other.

Bettyhill is in an unforgettable spot thirty-two miles west of Thurso and twelve miles from Tongue. The road takes you over the River Naver, from where you can see spits of pale gold stretching like fingers out to sea. As I didn't have Jussi's address, just a vague set of directions, I was keeping a keen look out for goats in a landscape that seemed to be all about sheep. Eventually I stopped at the village store to ask if they could help me and was pleased to see Jussi's cheeses neatly lined up inside the chiller cabinet. With the aid of a little map quickly scrawled on the back of a till receipt, I was soon on my way again. I just hoped that Jussi would be in. My plan to call ahead to advise her of my visit had been stymied due to a lack of mobile phone reception.

Bambi bounced up a long stony track and then over the brow of a hill, from where I finally spied a smattering of goats in shades of bronze, brown and cream grazing in the fields ahead. Surely this must be it? I parked a little way up from the farm, jumped out and made my way to the door. A jolly man answered my hesitant knock. 'You must be Kathleen's friend!' He laughed, shook my hand warmly and introduced himself as Jussi's husband, Simon. It seemed that Kathleen had called ahead to say I might be stopping by and so my appearance on their doorstep hadn't come entirely out of the blue.

I was ushered into the kitchen for a welcome cup of tea where we waited for Jussi to return from a couple of errands. We were soon joined by seventeen-year-old Ailsa, just back from walking a very large and affectionate dog. Ailsa, it seemed, had not been entirely enthusiastic about her mother's determination to move to the back of beyond to become a goat farmer, but with university just a welcome year away, she had a get-out plan up her sleeve. Unlike her daughter, however, Jussi was relishing her life far from the madding crowd, and on returning home she greeted me like an old friend, immediately decking me out in a pair of wellies, eager to introduce me to her herd.

I'd been told that goats can be rather stubborn and unfriendly, but these animals were gorgeous, with long silky ears and shaggy coats. They immediately capered over to greet their mistress who knew them all by name. Each animal wore a different coloured ribbon round its neck, but I had the impression that Jussi would have been able to tell her goats apart even if she was blindfolded.

She clearly adored her new job working the land, but was the first to admit that it wasn't without its challenges. Most people had farmed in the area for generations and had no real concept of what it was like for a stranger to set up a smallholding from scratch. Sheep were definitely the norm here and so initially Jussi's goats had been viewed with a great deal of suspicion. Financially it was tough too. Without Simon's income, they wouldn't have been able to make the change, and even several years into the enterprise they were still struggling to turn a profit. But Jussi had no regrets about her move and had just about managed to cement her reputation as a serious farmer.

She laughed as she told me about a rather macho local man who'd been booked to mend the fences and who'd made no bones at all about his lack of faith in her abilities. He was soon silenced, though, after watching Jussi round up her flock one evening without the need for a sheepdog. She just called her queen goat by name and all the others fell into line. The man couldn't believe how docile the animals were and how they'd obeyed Jussi's every command. From that moment, he scoffed no more and treated her with renewed respect.

Jussi and Simon kindly offered me supper and a bed for the night. I was sorely tempted, but I had to get a little further down south that evening, as I was due back in Montrose the following day. I knew from experience that too many hours sitting behind the wheel in Bambi always left me feeling tired and I didn't want to have to complete the journey in one go.

I headed off reluctantly and, following Simon's advice, made for the Strathnaver road, which cuts down the middle of the country. This one-track B road, which follows the course of the River Naver, seemed picturesque in the evening light, but in fact the area, like many parts of the Highlands, has an exceedingly dark history. At the beginning of the nineteenth century the Strathnaver valley sheltered about forty settlements, each housing a small number of families. In material terms, these communities were very poor. All tenants of the Countess of Sutherland, the people lived in basic dwellings constructed from local turf and eked out a living as cobblers, weavers, smithies or agricultural labourers. Their way of life had continued uninterrupted for generations, but it all changed when the Highland Clearances came to the valley in 1814 and then again in 1819. The houses were destroyed, families brutally evicted and scattered, and their small livings replaced by the large-scale sheep farms that have dominated the landscape ever since.

Today the sheep sector is a vital part of Scotland's economy – indeed there are many more sheep than people, a fact that hit home as I was brought to a standstill by a large flock being funnelled along the road by a Land Rover and two very enthusiastic dogs. On seeing Bambi (which must have looked like a UFO to them) the animals suddenly stopped moving and refused to budge, baaing loudly in protest. I pulled over into a passing place and switched off the engine, worried that I'd cause a stampede if I continued on. Bambi was soon surrounded on all four sides by nervous sheep, who jostled the van in their eagerness to get around it. It took around half an hour for the flock to be moved on, the farmer giving me a rather disapproving stare as he passed by. I'm sure that Bambi was the last thing he wanted to encounter at the end of a long, hard-working day.

Cathie

I needed to find somewhere to stop for the night, as it was getting a little late. Initially I thought about staying in the campsite near Altnaharra, but as I wasn't a Caravan Club member, it would have cost me £26 and there wasn't even a loo or shower. I decided to give it a miss and look for a cheaper option near Lairg. My journey continued down the Strath Bagastie road. The lush green valley that I'd been driving through eventually gave way to woodland, which soon became rather unlovely. Deforestation had left nasty scars, with felled trees, withered stumps and broken branches all creating the impression of a post-apocalyptic landscape. I carried on, feeling rather weary, finally seeing a sign for the Woodend Caravan Site, which took me down a small road about two miles off the main route. It was cold and drizzly and still only about 8 p.m., which meant a long evening ahead in the middle of nowhere.

The site consisted of a couple of very large fields and a functional-looking wash block. There was just one other visitor, a caravan parked way over in a lonely corner. I pulled up and followed the home-made sign to the reception desk, which was situated in the glass conservatory, a new addition to the traditional stone farmhouse. A smart elderly lady dressed in a satisfyingly old-fashioned jumper and reassuring tweed skirt appeared from a side door and informed me that it would cost £8 to stay the night. I couldn't argue with that – in fact it was the exact amount of cash I had left in my purse. Indicating the near-empty field she told me (without a hint of irony) that I could park anywhere I liked, so I got back into Bambi and drove onto the grass to find a suitable place to pull up. Moments later the rain started in earnest, quickly turning from a mild shower to a torrential downpour. Even heading outside to the loo a few metres away left me soaked through.

I tried my best to remain cheerful and attempted to make myself some supper with a few tomatoes, some basil, a ball of mozzarella and a surprise packet of out-of-date 'fresh' pasta, a souvenir from my time in Italy. Unearthing it I also discovered some shallots and limes that had been there for weeks. A distinct smell of mouldy vegetables pervaded Bambi and I wondered how I'd not noticed it before. I sat down to my meal accompanied by an old bottle of cider that quickly lost its fizz on pouring. It was all rather bleak. Even the view was a bit miserable. Loch Shin was a damp smudge through the window and the signs of further deforestation on the other side of the shore didn't exactly lift the spirits. I thought back to my night on Durness beach and wished I was still there. How quickly things can change. Ebb and flow. Ebb and flow. I wrote up my diary until it got dark and then turned in early for the night, putting on several layers, including a Shetland cardigan and three tartan blankets. Scotland in the summer.

I slept reasonably well in spite of the cold and damp, and by the time I surfaced it was getting on for nine o'clock in the morning. The sun was peering through the clouds and I felt a bit perkier. I decided to bypass a cooked breakfast and opted instead for a big mug of milky coffee brewed in my trusty Italian stove-top espresso maker. I paired the coffee with a peanut Tracker bar (my latest discovery), and soon I felt ready for the road again. It hadn't been the most memorable of stopovers, but the campsite had been clean and well kept. I had no real need to go and see the lady in the farmhouse, as I'd already settled up with her the night before. But something made me hesitate about driving off without saying goodbye.

It was one of those spur-of-the-moment decisions that brought unexpected rewards. Cathie Ross, who was eighty-two, turned out to be an excellent seamstress, a fact I only discovered once she'd glimpsed Bambi's home-made interior and recognised a kindred spirit. Like so many women of her generation, Cathie had clothed all four of her children herself by sewing, knitting and crocheting every single item in their wardrobes. Although she'd stopped doing that many years ago, she still loved making things and had continued sewing for pleasure all her life. She'd recently turned a decent profit at the village hall from her handmade aprons, book bags and peg bags. With a burst of enthusiasm she disappeared back to the house to fetch some of her creations to show me. She came back with a box full of neatly packed items, which she dismissed as 'being silly little things she just ran up for the sale'. They were, in fact, all beautifully made. Her peg bag (which had been constructed to resemble a small dress) reminded me of one I'd found at the flea market in Brussels. Soon Cathie was searching for a pen, newspaper and scissors to draw her peg-bag pattern for me and together we cut one out. She then went to rummage around for something else and returned with a length of tartan, unpicked a stitch at a time from an old kilt and pressed to perfection by her daughter-in-law. Cathie had used some of the same fabric to make a very posh peg bag, which she'd fashioned into a mini Highland outfit, complete with a sporran sewn from scraps of leather. This grand creation had been sent all the way to Australia as a gift. Cathie kindly offered me what was left of her tartan as well as the paper pattern. I was so touched that I gave her one of my signed books in return.

I finally waved goodbye to Cathie an hour later than I'd intended and drove back to the main road. It had been such a lovely encounter, particularly as it had followed such a dreary night. There are rich seams of creativity to be found in the most unexpected of places. Cathie had greeted me with such generosity of spirit. I hurtled towards Inverness and onwards towards Montrose, mindful that I had to get back there in time to clean my brother's house for the arrival of imminent guests.

The mountains rolled by, mellowing as I made my way further south, passing Bridge of Avon, Glenlivet, Cock Bridge and on through the Cairngorms National Park, which was peppered with out-of-season ski stations. The roads felt very quiet. I'd stupidly forgotten to top up with fuel and the needle was quickly nudging towards empty. Did I never learn?! It was sheer luck that I spotted a sign to Aboyne twelve miles away, where I sputtered into a petrol station, the tank almost dry. I motored on, following the glens where I used to go swimming as a child, until I reached Fettercairn and the Cairn O' Mount viewpoint. From there I could marvel at the parcelled-up farmland of Angus and Aberdeenshire spread out like a patchwork blanket before dipping away into the sea. A never-ending bolt of fabric in myriad shades of grey, green and blue.

Back in Montrose, a friend gave me an old blanket that she no longer wanted. On closer inspection I discovered that it was a 'national price-controlled blanket' with a label to prove it, a relic of post-Second World War rationing – a treasure in my eyes. I'd loved the fact that Cathie had requisitioned the kilt fabric for her peg bags and I was keen to use my blanket for an upcycling project too. The blanket was 100 per cent wool and still in reasonable condition, bar a few stains and moth holes. It was too good to cut into small pieces, but no longer useful on a bed. I decided to try making a little travelling cloak, a capelet that could be embellished as and when inspiration struck. A blank canvas that would look good plain but would gain character over time.

The great thing about old blankets is that they're often fairly felted from use and therefore don't need much in the way of hemming. In fact, shortly after acquiring my friend's blanket, I came across a whole pile of ex-navy ones in a Montrose charity shop. They'd been discovered on board a Norwegian trawler that was off to the broker's yard and were going for a song at £3 each. I bought five, excited to find such a rare prize. These military blankets came in various shades of brown and khaki, practical, robust and although a little damaged in places, perfect for turning into covetable accessories. My travelling cape is pretty simple to make, as it's essentially a circle with a hole in the middle for your head. You can tweak it in different ways to give it a different look. I've created versions with a stand-up collar, no collar, and the rather romantic one I've included here, which ties at the front in a big bow made from contrasting fabric. Don't be afraid to improvise and try different styles yourself. Capes make a great foil for embroidery, whether you want to write political slogans or depict birds and flowers. You can also sew on travel patches or old Guide/Scout badges to create a kind of outdoor camping-rug feel. Indeed, my capes sometimes double as something to sit on when I'm out for a picnic! In short, a cape is endlessly useful, and together with the top and skirt from earlier in the book, a home-made cape completes your capsule travelling ensemble.

Make a Romantic Travelling Cape

You can make this cape any size. Simply measure from the edge of your neck down your arm to figure out the length you want and add on an extra 7cm to allow for the hole in the middle (you can always adjust this if you wish). I used furnishing fabric to make the neckline bow as it's really strong material and will take the weight of the blanket. This is a sewing-machine project. See the photo in the colour plates.

You'll need

- a measuring tape
- string and a fabric-marker pen or chalk
- an old blanket (the more felted ones work well, as they won't fray)
- contrasting fabric for the bow (cotton furnishing fabric is a good choice)
- an iron
- sewing machine, scissors, pins, needle and thread
- bobble trim to decorate (the amount you need will depend on the circumference of your cape)

How to make

1. Measure from the edge of your neck down the side of your arm to give you the length of your cape. Add on another 7 cm to allow for your head. Cut a piece of string this length, plus a little extra so you can tie it onto your pen or onto the chalk.

2. Fold your blanket into quarters and use the string like a compass anchored at the corner to draw a quarter-circle pattern onto it. Then shorten the string to 7 cm and draw another smaller quarter circle for the neckline (see diagram). Cut out along both lines, then slice down one of the folded edges to create the front opening.

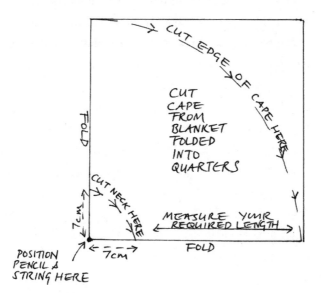

CUT EDGE OF CAPE HERE

CUT
CAPE
FROM
BLANKET
FOLDED
INTO
QUARTERS

FOLD

CUT NECK HERE

7cm

MEASURE YOUR
REQUIRED LENGTH

FOLD

POSITION
PENCIL &
STRING HERE

7cm

3. Zigzag the edges to prevent fraying if necessary and stay stitch round the neckline edge to stop it stretching. Measure round your neckline and mark the centre back (opposite the front opening).

4. Now for the bow. You'll probably need to make it in two sections, as it's long and generous. The fabric for my bow measured 250 cm long and 26 cm wide. Fold in half lengthways (right sides together) to form a tube, pin to hold it all together and cut the ends at an angle. Mark the centre back.

5. Now divide the cape's neckline measurement in half and put a mark this length on the bow either side of the centre back (I always add in a couple of extra centimetres to allow for a margin of error). Sew all the way around the edges of

the bow starting and finishing at the two marks you've just made. Turn the right way out and press.

6. Now pin the centre back of the cape's neckline to the centre back of one of the sides of the bow fabric (right sides of the cape and the bow together). Pin on carefully, easing the neckline into the gap in the bow as necessary and tacking into place. Finally, machine stitch together and remove the tacking stitches. NB – You'll finish the neckline off once you've attached your trim, as you'll need to tuck the trim inside for a neat finish.

7. Attach your bobble trim all the way around the outside edges of the cape using a matching thread (cut off any little pom-poms that get in the way of the neckline edge).

8. To finish off, fold the remaining side of the bow in place over the neckline, tucking the blanket inside and trimming back any pom-poms that get in the way. Fold under the raw edge of the bow. Pin together and hand stitch the seam, closing any little gaps on either side of the collar at the same time.

21

Endings and Beginnings

And so, now that we're fully dressed for the journey, we ironically near the end of my book. I stayed up in Montrose for another season. September saw the fields shorn, gold filigree buttons of hay punctuating the rough stubble. October heralded skeins of pink-footed geese, who stitched the sky with their outstretched wings. Another Christmas came and went, marked by more writing and a few seasonal pop-ups and fairs. I started doing the farmers' market in Montrose on a regular basis – my Shetland jumpers were just what people needed to help keep the bitter north wind at bay. Soon nearly all my family and friends owned at least one – it became a kind of sweater club! I rented trestle tables in chilly church halls, gave talks to local branches of the Women's Institute and ran a Burns Night craft workshop at a friend's house, warmed by her roaring log fire. Then my lodger in London left. Without that income I couldn't continue in Scotland indefinitely. Money was running very low.

There was nothing for it but to go back to my flat, find a job urgently and pick up the thread of my old life. It was, if I'm honest, a huge anticlimax, an enforced farewell that had come far too soon. I felt I'd been unable to tie the various strands of the last couple of years together in the way that I'd wanted. I'd hoped to deliver a big gift box to myself, complete with resplendent bow, and I was going to have to forego that for the time being. But what *was* that gift box a symbol of anyway? Maybe it was about allowing myself to become an artist instead of a hard-nosed journalist. I'd not once regretted my decision to leave behind the world of hourly deadlines and the daily diet of bad news. I sensed that the newsroom had become a distraction, a way of avoiding confronting my hopes and dreams in case I couldn't pull them off. Setting out on my journey in Bambi had been a risky leap of faith, a scary thing to do. But I'd learned so much by doing it. I now knew that I wanted to live a simpler, more creative life, in tune with nature – my travels had definitely shown me that. But I hadn't yet found a way of balancing this new life and making it pay. It would take time. So on a cold February morning I packed Bambi up once again, bade farewell to Scotland and regretfully headed back down the road to London. On the surface, nothing had changed, yet everything was different.

I still don't know exactly what I'm reaching for, but things have certainly moved on. Since returning to London I've given up news journalism completely and am currently curating and running a community shop and gallery on behalf of a local charitable organisation. We sell the work of more than sixty artists and craftspeople and run workshops teaching a variety of skills. I've discovered that the artists I work with are on a creative course of their own too and we help each other along the path. As I write this, I'm planning a permanent move to the coast and I'm finally publishing this book. Things will change again. Ultimately, it's the journey and the making of it that counts, not the end goal. We're constantly reshaping our own landscape.

Make Your Own Vintage Curtains

It's time to let the curtain fall on what we shall call Act One, and appropriately, I have a curtain project for you.

My curtains are very simple to make. I sewed them up in Scotland during the winter from a large dust sheet that my cousin had saved from the school bin. After washing it, I discovered it was made of a wonderful thick cheesecloth type of fabric with a heavy drape that nonetheless filtered the light beautifully.

I picked out the best vintage doilies from my collection and hand stitched them on to the sheet one by one. It took some time, but it was worth it. You can also use a sewing machine to help speed up the process.

The curtain is hung with special clips that have rings attached so you can slip them onto a pole. Ingenious! This curtain gives me great joy. In certain lights the doilies look just like stencils that have been painted on rather than stitched. I think of each one as a miniature work of art. See the photo in the colour plates.

You'll need

- a sheet or plain voile curtain
- a selection of vintage crochet doilies
- pins
- needle and thread
- hanging clips

How to make

1. Lay your sheet or curtain flat on the floor and pin your doilies into position so you can plan your design (I like a very random look).
2. Next, hang up the fabric if you can, as it's easier to sew that way. If you can't hang it just yet, drape it over a sofa or door.
3. Put a knot at the end of a longish thread and sew each doily into position one by one, using small stitches that pierce through the doily on the front, and large stitches on the back that enable you to work your way around the doily fairly quickly. Hanging your curtain allows you to see where the doilies sag and need stitching down.
4. You can make this over a period of time. Sew on extra doilies when the mood takes you, so it can be a work in progress... very much like our lives.

To get your bearings, you must
Stop. Look. Listen.
Stay alert for that still small voice,
The one that will help you find your heart
And finally lead you home.

Mary Jane Baxter

Index of 'Makes'

Acknowledgements

I would like to thank my dear friends, my lovely family and my fantastic colleagues at GCDA for their incredible support and generosity over the last few years. My brother Anthony and my friends Mel, Steve, Gary and Jonathan have been particularly kind, putting me up in their homes when I've needed a place to stay. I really appreciate it.

This book couldn't have happened without the creative input of the Unbound team, particularly Katy Guest, who kept me on track during the crowdfunding stage and Anna Simpson, my hardworking editor, without whom I couldn't have wrestled this book into submission.

Thank you to all those I met, stayed with and spoke to during my journey – your enthusiasm and kindness meant such a lot to me.

Most of all, huge thanks to all of you who pledged so generously to help this book see the light of day. I'm so grateful for and humbled by your support.

Mary Jane Baxter, March 2021
www.maryjanemakes.co.uk

Unbound is the world's first crowdfunding publisher, established in 2011.

We believe that wonderful things can happen when you clear a path for people who share a passion. That's why we've built a platform that brings together readers and authors to crowdfund books they believe in – and give fresh ideas that don't fit the traditional mould the chance they deserve.

This book is in your hands because readers made it possible. Everyone who pledged their support is listed below. Join them by visiting unbound.com and supporting a book today.

Barry Abbott

Melanie Abbott

Sarah Abel

Carol Ackroyd

Julia Adamson

Liz Aldous

Ruth Alexander

Eli Allison

Elaine Andersen

Sue Anstiss

Stephanie Arnold

Penny Ashton

Michelle Aslett

Natalie Atkins-Sloan

Becky Balai

Louise Baltes

Valerie Banks

Paula Barder

Andy Barnard

Anthony Baxter

Chris Baxter

Emma Bayliss

Charlotte Benvie

Guillaume Bertrand

Dave Betts

Emma Bilde Carp

Sandra Bilde Carp

Tom Birrell

Graham Black

Jodie Black

Stephen Bloy

Ann Booth

Sara Booth

Lesley Bower

Jennifer Broadley

Broderie_Solange

Kelvin Brown

Martina Bunker

Emma Cameron

Jennie Caminada

Kim Canale

Jill Cansell

Caroline Casson

Gemma Champ

Jane Charity

Ashley Charlton

Katharina Child

Jo Christofides

Cathy Clarke

Philippa Coates

Mindy Collins

Sofia Connolly

Sarah Cordingley

Philippe Couineaux

Dada Neon

EJ Davies

Julia Davies

Marcello De Vitis

Ann De Waele

Sheila Dillon

Martha Dixon

Dr Jonathan Douglas CBE and
Gary Mack

Jane Downes

Malcolm Downing

Rachel Drewer

Katy Driver

Fiona Duncan

David Dunford

Helen Edwards

Danielle Ellis

Gwilym Ellis

Susan Emmett

The lovely Sue Facherty

Barbara Farrell

Anne-Katrin Fischer

Flamingo Arts

Sean Flood

Eimear Flynn

Gwenda & Zelda Forbes

Babette Forsyth

Gina Foster

Martin Foulds

Nicola Frost

Helen Fryers

Akane Furukawa

Antonia Galloway

Timothy Gauntley

Sinead Geary

Nicola Gibson

Geoff Goff

Nickos Gogolos

Jane Gois

Natasha Goodfellow

Heide Goody

Charlotte Goulette

Aki Gourdandhorse

Talitha Graham

Peter Grant

Morag Gray

Nick Gray

Ann Griese

Rhona Grieve

Cathy Griffiths

Fiona Guest

Lynn Hall

Jacqui Harding

Andrea Harman

Aine Haslam

Jess Hawker Meadley

Carol Hay

Chloe Haywood

Mary Hearne

Allie Henderson

Kathleen Henderson

Susannah Henry Wood

Emma Hickey

Rebecca Hindle

Lucy Hodges

Catherine Hopewell

Sarah Hosking

Irene Hughes

Diana Hurley

Helen Ingham

Krassimira Ivanova

Elena Jackson

Maureen Jackson
Jane Fryers Millinery
Alison Jeffers
Sarah Jenner
Lottie Johansson
Bill Jones
Nancy Jones
Simone Keeley
Suzanne Kelly
Dan Kieran
Samantha King
Sue King
Caroline Kinghorn
Manuela Kipper
Emma Jane Kirby
Sean Klein
Deb Knowles
Inka Kretschmer
Livia La Camera
Elizabeth Laidler
Jhennia Leipert
Caroline Lewis
Aileen Loney
Louisa Loney
Oana Lungescu
Norma Lyall
Emma Macalister Hall
Fiona Maida

Jennifer Mair
Frances Marnie
John Marshman
Jan Martin
Ursula Mayr
Ailsa McCarthy
Megan McCormick
Helen McElwee
Sue McFarlane
John McManus
Katya Menshikova
Judy Merrill-Smith
Liz Merryweather
Patricia Milling
John Mitchinson
Amanda Moron-Garcia
Avila Murray
John Murray
Josephine Murray
Delphine Musy El Atouani
Carlo Navato
Caroline Nuttall-Smith
Ellen Oberhart
Davina Osborn
Vita Osborne
Peter Owen
Kat P.
Brian Palmer

Nicky Parkinson
Freya Parson
Kat Parsons
Lynda Paton
Julie Pearce
Annabel Pearcey
Esme Pears
Rosie Pepper
Andy Phelps
Lucilla Phelps
Rupert Phelps
Gordon Phillips
Liz Phillips
Yvette Pitchforth
Justin Pollard
Alison Powell
Liz Powner
Ian and Cathy Poyser
Elaine Pretty
Claire Pritchard
Melanie Pritchard
Jane Raffaele Krause
Anne Ransford
Alba Reavley
Sue Redgrift
Betty Redondo
Sue Reekie
Clare Rhodes James

Denis Rice
Dominic & Theresa Rice
Paula Rice
Diane Roberts
Stephanie Robinson
Melissa Rochoux
Christopher Roe
Katy Roelich
Heather Rosa
Robin Ross
Keira Esse Roth
Mike Salloway
Gemma Sangwine
Victoria Sangwine-Gould
Michael Scorgie
Kirsten Scott
Pam Seaby
Rebecca Seibel
Jill Sentance
Sew and Sew
Andrew Shead
Chris Simmonds
Lisa Small
Catherine Smillie
Kerry Smith
Duncan Snelling
Greta Snipe
Claire Snodgrass

Lili Soh
Alison Souter
Pascale Spall
Andrew Spencer
Ruth Spencer
Josephine Steed
Elly Stemerdink
Jennifer Stilwell
Eliza Stuart
Katy Styles
Janine Sullivan
Sam Sutherland
Anne-Marie Swift
Orsi Szoboszlay
Helen Tate
Ruth Taylor
Jillian Tees
Rachel Thomas
Simon Thomson
Dr Lorna Tinworth
Catherine Toole
Leonie Vatter
Yolanda Vega
Bernice Walker
Anna Wallace
Caroline Wallace
Sheila Wallace
Jennie Waters

Lara Watson
Teresa Watts
Sofia Wendler
Sandra Westbrooke
Katie Weston
Sarah Whitehead
Fay Williams
Sarah Willoughby
Niamh Wilson
Jane Wintersgill
Georgina Worthington
Rene Wyndham Sweeney
J L Yates
Liz Zass